Healing
through the
Eyes *of a* Woman

© Copyright 2007 Alison Feather Adams.
All rights reserved. No part of this publication may be reproduced, stored in a retrieval system, or transmitted, in any form or by any means, electronic, mechanical, photocopying, recording, or otherwise, without the written prior permission of the author.

Note for Librarians: A cataloguing record for this book is available from Library and Archives Canada at www.collectionscanada.ca/amicus/index-e.html
ISBN 1-4251-1487-3

Printed in Victoria, BC, Canada. Printed on paper with minimum 30% recycled fibre. Trafford's print shop runs on "green energy" from solar, wind and other environmentally-friendly power sources.

Offices in Canada, USA, Ireland and UK

Book sales for North America and international:
Trafford Publishing, 6E–2333 Government St.,
Victoria, BC V8T 4P4 CANADA
phone 250 383 6864 (toll-free 1 888 232 4444)
fax 250 383 6804; email to orders@trafford.com

Book sales in Europe:
Trafford Publishing (UK) Limited, 9 Park End Street, 2nd Floor
Oxford, UK OX1 1HH UNITED KINGDOM
phone +44 (0)1865 722 113 (local rate 0845 230 9601)
facsimile +44 (0)1865 722 868; info.uk@trafford.com

Order online at:
trafford.com/06-3246

10 9 8 7 6 5 4 3

Healing *through the* Eyes *of a* Woman

Reconnecting with Intuition to Heal the Self

ALISON FEATHER ADAMS

Contents

Preface	7
Intuition is a Common Sense We have Forsaken	17
Embracing a New Perspective	47
The Process of Inner Alchemy	71
Case Studies	161
Finding Our Way Back to the Origin	191
Integrating the Feminine	237
Acknowledgements	251

Preface

This book is about reconnecting with the feminine energy of intuition to heal the Self, so there is nothing separating you, from perceiving the truth of who you really are, in your potential. It is through my own personal journey as a woman, and the privilege of working with my patients in my clinical practice of Auricular and Bioenergetic Medicine that I have come to understand how as individuals we heal, not only on the physical level, but on the emotional and mental levels as well. These are my perceptions as a woman, through the exploration in awareness of the feminine energy of intuition, living in a world where our traditional roles and expression of who we are is being challenged by our need to grow, and go beyond what has been defined for us by society. It has been through my clinical experience that I have come to apply my Medical Intuitive abilities, and to articulate the Process of Inner Alchemy, to help others realize within themselves the power of intuition, to heal what conventional medicine has failed to acknowledge as a vital component in reclaiming their health. The Process of Inner Alchemy involves working intuitively with our body, mind and Spirit, to transform all that no longer serves to support our true state of health and wellbeing.

After participating in a Qigong retreat in the Philippines, where I treated some of the people attending, I was asked if I would consider doing a workshop to teach them what I was doing. At that time, I had not defined or structured the Process of Inner Alchemy, as you find it here, as I was strictly working intuitively in conjunction with Auricular Medicine. I was apprehensive about teaching my work with intuition at first, because it meant that I had to bring forward the part of myself, that was much more comfortable working intimately within the sanctuary of my office. The group that gathered in Spain consisted of my husband Mikhael, and four others. That workshop in Spain was an incredible experience, not only because of witnessing the emergence of the intuitive gifts of each of the group members, but also because I came to define the Process of Inner Alchemy. While traveling to Spain, we had a stopover at Heathrow Airport, and when we took a walk outside, a rash started to appear on my hands. By the time we got to our final destination, that rash was not only covering my hands, but there was a patch on the side of my nose, on my cheek, and up my arms. It was really itchy, red and inflamed, and it was being further aggravated by exposure to the sun. For the next four days, I had the irritation of this rash annoying me, and I could not figure out what it was about. I didn't recognize it, nor did anyone else. I ignored it the best I could, and placed my focus on showing the group how to tap into their subtler senses to do Medical Intuitive Scans.

On the fourth day, I was working with Sarah, who had not only inspired the gathering, but had organized getting us all to their home up in the remote hills of Ibiza, Spain, from Portugal, the Netherlands, and Mikhael and I from Canada. She had supported and encouraged me to come and "work live," as she put it, without feeling any pressure from anyone to define a structure of teaching it perfectly. Everyone gathered was committed to helping me find my voice in teaching Medical intuition. When we had first arrived, Sarah's husband had shown us his book collection from his years of study, and had shared with us his love of the *I Ching, Book of Change*. He had offered, that if I would like to make use of any of his books while I was there, I was welcome. That fourth day, four of us stayed behind, while he and another from the group went to swim in the ocean nearby. I asked if I might borrow a copy of his *I Ching, Book of Change*, to work with while they were gone. The rest of us sat outside in the shade, and Sarah and I had engaged in sharing how intuition can reveal depth to our current perceptions of ourselves facing challenge. I pulled out the *I Ching* to consult after we had launched into a particular topic, and had intuitively explored the origins of our perceptions. She threw the pennies and we looked up the trigrams in the book to see what clarity might further be revealed. As we looked up the indicated trigram, I shared how I work with external resources intuitively by honing in on one of the paragraphs. I was playfully showing her how we can hone in on relevant passages in reference books, when looking for clarity, by using our inner senses to find frequencies that resonate with our body energy. By using our inner senses, we can bypass our current perceptions, and understanding, to tap into the body wisdom, which has the ability to take us to clarity, that might not otherwise be consciously recognized as relevant to us. Sure enough, the very things we had unveiled intuitively were referenced in those pages very clearly, in different verbiage. I was reading an excerpt for the book aloud when her husband arrived back from the beach. He was livid at finding me reading excerpts from his book, and hearing our casual exchange about how hearing wisdom expressed differently, can shed further light on what intuitively we perceive, but have little experience in expressing. I wasn't making fun of the book, or intuition, it was simply enjoying learning with one another. His energy might as well have been a knife delivered straight into my heart. He was angry because he felt that I was being irreverent to the years of study and ethics required to work with the *I Ching*, and that the joy and playfulness in my approach to working with the sacred in general, was completely irresponsible. It was a barrage that in my openness in that moment, had completely devastated me. We were all a little in shock, but for me, it had reduced me to not being able to communicate with words at all. I was unable to speak, taking in his opinion and understanding of me out of respect for being a guest in his home. I couldn't find my voice, but I felt tears well up from within me and I sat there quietly feeling like my essence was exposed as the tears began to flow. At that moment, there were no words to justify or explain myself, the tears were the only expression that came welling up from inside me, and they felt very inadequate. There was no turning it off or hiding it. I had been truly comfortable with Sarah, and the others in our work together, that I had been openly sharing my true self. It was a mutual exchange, and spontaneous, because we were all freely expressing our perceptions that afternoon. In that moment, I wished that I had stayed at home and kept to myself what I knew and believed. I felt I had been caught doing what is the most natural thing in me, and that it felt wrong because it was now in the open to be criticized. I was sharing with them how I utilize resources that can help clarify what we know intuitively, but have a hard time recognizing in ourselves. In essence, the great lesson being offered to me was an appreciation for how unique our individual perceptions can be of the very same thing!

One of the other women who had been part of our *I Ching* exchange, who was the most unassuming and gentle of the group, spoke up and shared what she was feeling. She was grateful I had agreed to come and share my knowledge with her. She asserted herself, and pointed out that maybe he didn't know what was going on, because he hadn't been present for the whole thing. She very calmly suggested to him that possibly things were not as they seemed. He remained angry, and retreated into the house, wanting nothing to do with anyone in that moment, and especially me. I was feeling dismissed by his display of authority. Mikhael was the only other man there, and he gently put his hand on my knee, completely unemotional about what had happened, but I felt his understanding of what was going on in that situation. His many years of lecturing and teaching had already given him this experience, and he recognized it was something I had the strength to deal with myself. Five of us remained outside in complete silence.

There was nowhere to retreat to, and nowhere to be alone that day. We were up in the hills, miles from anything, without transpor-

Preface

tation for a reason, because otherwise, in that moment of discomfort, I would have packed my bags and caught a flight out of there! I had to stay... What I did next was turn my chair to face Mikhael, because I trusted him to just hold sacred space for me for a few moments. My rash was driving me crazy, and now I felt completely at a loss to know how to proceed. As I sat facing Mikhael, I allowed myself to really feel the hurt and upset of that moment. With my eyes closed, tears running down my face, I went right into the feelings within me, surrendering to them knowing I had support do this for myself. I spoke aloud, as I went through the process. In my current state, I felt like I was six years old again, and as soon as I surrendered to my feelings of complete shame, it was as if I was right back in the middle of an incident that had happened at that age. At six, I had spontaneously expressed myself, and out of my mouth I had called someone 'nosey'. I remembered this incident, except that in this moment, I was that young girl again, and it wasn't the way I had remembered it exactly. I didn't know then what being 'nosey' meant. This man had been joking, and having fun with my brother and sister and I, and in my innocence, I had gotten completely caught up in his fun loving nature. I had called him nosey because he had a big nose, and as he talked, he was doing funny things with his nose to play with me. After blurting out that he was nosey, my father reacted so fast, I didn't know what was happening. We were in the car at the time, giving this man a ride home from church. The adults were in the front seat, and my brother, sister and I, in the back seat. My father immediately pulled off to the shoulder of the highway, got out of the car and came around and opened my car door. He pulled me out of the car, and there on the side of the road, up went my dress, and down went my pants, and he gave me a spanking. My father told me sternly never to call anyone that again. It all happened so fast I didn't know what had happened exactly. I wondered for a long time after that, what was wrong with what I had said. I was afraid to ask, because I knew it meant something really bad, and that I would be punished for even mentioning it. I was humiliated, but more importantly, I had decided it wasn't safe to spontaneously express myself. My father was a good man, and never intended to hurt me, he genuinely loved me and I wasn't afraid of him, but I respected him and was careful not to disappoint him in front of company. He was operating from the accepted norm of that time that endorsed spanking as the proper way to discipline your children. Though a child, I was a young lady in his eyes, and expected to have manners and respect for my elders at all times. I just happened to be very sensitive, and it was easier to just be quiet, and to keep my thoughts to myself, than face being misunderstood and humiliated again. I hadn't actually thought about this incident in many years, and certainly had no idea that I had made a decision about myself way back then that had brought me to be very careful and quiet about my internal perceptions. I spent most my time alone growing up, and groups of people made me uncomfortable, especially if I had to stand up spontaneously, and share something of myself with them. To this day, time alone is very rejuvenating for me. I have always been very organized and prepared when dealing with others, so I would avoid being humiliated through spontaneously responding, even if it was from my heart. Up until that day in Spain, I hadn't realized that decision about myself had influenced so many decisions I went on to make through my life. I actually unknowingly avoided expressing my intuitive abilities for many years because of this underlying fear.

In going to Spain, I was accepting an invitation to step out of my comfort zone, to share how I worked intuitively. It is when I am relaxed, and playful, that intuitively the information is right there for me. It is not irreverence; it's authentically the way I am. Intuitively perceived information has the ability to trigger people who are highly educated, and have studied extensively philosophy and psychology. To have someone like me show up who says, "this is easy, everyone can do this if you stop thinking about it, relax and listen to what comes naturally without censoring!" The truth is, that it has taken me years of working with this internally, and summoning the courage to be out with it, because of how it is often received by the intellect. This is about feeling, and knowing through sensing. That has been my personal challenge, and reason for avoiding authority. I approach and know things differently.

I am not an expert, nor have I ever claimed to be. I can't scientifically explain or justify how I am able to read energy, and receive information about an individual's health, or how they have come to express their state of disease within themselves. I can share with you how I do it though, and you'll realize that you too perceive intuitively, without realizing it as *real*. I have no interest in proving it. I would rather invest my time helping others cultivate their own intuitive skills, and facilitating them to integrate their own intuitive abilities, with who they really are, not just with what they do, or the roles they have come to define themselves by, in their life.

Medical Intuition is what I do, it is not who I am. I am intuitive, but so is everyone else... it's in our essence to intuitively perceive. I share this experience of my first time teaching Medical Intuition, because it was a profound step, and learning experience for me. Everyone in Spain could do a scan by day two, and it became very obvious that in doing this work, we are all faced with ourselves, to heal in some way. I sat down and wrote down the process I had done, to heal the hurt and pain inside myself, from that confrontation. The current situation was not the problem, it was the perception of a long time ago, when I was a child that had kicked in and made it impossible for me to speak my truth, in the current moment. Having healed it within myself, I was able to come to an honest understanding of my part in the current exchange, and the others in the group in turn, were moved to honestly come forward, with how they had experienced it. We all grew and healed in our own way during that time together.

As Mikhael had sat quietly, and listened to me in this process, my emotions had shifted to reveal clarity. The name of a homeopathic remedy came to me, as I had defined my part in the experience, and realized the relationship between the original incident, and the confrontation, I had experienced. It was a necessary part of myself that needed liberating, in order to stand my ground, in the presence of acknowledged authority. The remedy was Rhus Toxicodendron, and with that realization, the annoyance with my rash became clear, because I had Poison Ivy. The natural properties of Poison Ivy resonated with the greatest fear this part of Self wanted me to recognize, and heal, in order to move forward with what I had been asked to teach. The authority within myself, at the level of Soul, needed to be recognized, in regards to working intuitively. None of us as doctors recognized this unique expression of Poison Ivy. I took the homeopathic remedy, and within an hour the rash had calmed down and no longer bothered me. By nightfall the rash had completely resolved. I wasn't a threatened child anymore. Instead, I was reunited with the innocent child within that facilitates working intuitively, without inhibition. The anger of that moment had separated Sarah's husband from receiving the best part of what I was sharing that day, trusting ones ability to be spontaneously guided by intuitive energy. In not recognizing this part of Self that had been triggered by his accusation, I had lost my ability to see past his anger, to hear him clearly in his hurt. He was a scholar, and his work with the *I Ching* was obviously more comprehensive than what we were utilizing, within the context of that situation. In being guided intuitively, I was utilizing the book as a tool, through resonating with body wisdom, not my intellect, which would have honored the complete embodiment of that book, in a different way. They are both worthy, and valid approaches, in utilizing information, to help us in our search for clarity. When in harmony, they both can bring depth to understanding, and in turn strengthen the bond between the wisdom of the heart, and the knowledge of the intellect.

Embracing the feminine energy within can call forward many limitations, which our life experience has endorsed for us. In following

Preface

Spirit, we are relinquishing our personal authority in situations, in order to embrace a greater truth that is revealed to us, through our subtle senses. The authority we follow is within the energy of each individual's body, and how it is uniquely expressing its disease state. The seed for actualizing the Process of Inner Alchemy was planted with that special group of people in Spain, to help me find my voice, for what was in my Soul to share. That was the potential unveiled, but not fully realized, during our time together. I had been working on this process privately for some time, but the opportunity to speak it out loud, and share my approach, had brought potential to what I would go on to work with, and further define, with the help of others.

Our angels appear in many disguises, so with courage, we sometimes have to trust, and let our essence be revealed, so Spirit can guide us past our limited current perceptions, to find our authentic True Self again. The gift of defining Inner Alchemy, as a process that others can do, is to be able to nurture the feminine principles of intuition, in a language that enables others to hear the part of Self inside them, that is yearning to be recognized, and healed. It is in our healing of Self, that we are free to come forward as a fuller, truer expression of who we really are, with the power of transformation that our Soul unveils, through our humanness. This book is not about women, or specifically for women, rather a guide to begin working with the principles of the feminine energy of intuition, as expressed by a woman.

PART ONE:

Intuition is a Common Sense We have forsaken

*I*ntuition is sensing on a subtle energetic level, that which is beyond the experience of the five senses of touch, sight, smell, taste and hearing, as we have come to experience them in our physical body. For each of the five developed senses, there are subtle senses that every living thing also has. As a matter of fact, we come into this world as newborn babies, with the subtle senses being our only developed means of sensing, and knowing ourselves.

During the formative years we learn to navigate the physical world by developing our physical senses of touch, smell, taste, sight and hearing, in relation to our physical body, as it grows and develops. We learn as children to master these body based senses, to care for our physical bodies, by making the connections between what we naturally perceive through subtle energy, and what we experience with the physical senses. We *learn* that fire can burn our fingers. We learn how to perceive depth, so we don't fall down stairs. We learn our limitations within the physical body, through the mastering of the tools we have been given, in the human form. Our hands, ears, mouths, eyes and noses are all explored, in their ability to discern our physicality, and the pathways of communication between them, and our brains, teach us how to discern what they represent. We also *learn* acceptable expression of our creativity, our ideas, and our dreams, and adapt these expressions, based on how others respond to us. These conceptual expressions of our experiences get put under the umbrella of imagination, and we learn to describe them as *not real*.

During those first few years we come to redefine our experience of who we are based on external references. To physically survive, we adopt the customs, and behaviors that keep us safe, within our environment. We are reliant on caregivers to meet our needs, until we have developed skills to care for ourselves in the physical form. Hand in hand with the physicality of our experience, come the imprints of beliefs and values that our environment provides for us, through demonstration. Our caregivers, and significant people in our life, show us and impart to us their methods, their ways of seeing, and being in this reality, without us even realizing it. The boundaries of who we are, and every other living thing, come into existence for us as we develop our physical skills.

As newborns we are one with all, and the concept of separateness doesn't yet exist for us, because we haven't yet come to experience any boundaries, energetic or physical. Those that love us also automatically share with us, how to handle ourselves in various situations, and we develop ways of responding to others, and our environment, based on the models we are exposed to. We unknowingly become a synthesis, of what we adopt consciously and unconsciously from others, and what we are in Essence from the beginning of existence. Often, our subtle sensing is overshadowed, by the process of becoming engaged in the physicality of life situations. So, from the day of birth into this reality, our focus is brought from a place of Being One with All, to an awareness of Self, in relationship to the physical vessel we know as our bodies. As we mature, our internal world once again starts to become aware of its Self, and we begin the process of understanding the external world, in relation to ourselves. This process of integration is where we meet our challenges of self-actualization. The challenge becomes, to take the learned illusion of separation, and integrating it with the innate knowledge of a greater reality of our being, that is Oneness with All.

Have you ever wondered if there is more? Something beyond what you currently are experiencing? As humans we are being moved to a deeper experience of ourselves. It is like a call to come home from somewhere deep inside us. It never ceases and will find ways to have itself heard by us. There is no validation externally that can quantify it, nor define it in a way that can explain or prove it beyond a doubt.

It is beyond explanation in the realm of rationalism. I am not talking about a bigger house, more money, wealth and prosperity in concrete form. I am talking about inner peace, vitality, wellbeing, and joy for life. For some, it is not until these concrete demonstrations are satisfied, that we are left to face that feeling, that there is still something fundamental missing for us. The part that is missing can't be filled by anything outward, and as long as we try to satisfy it with acquiring things, we continually return to the feeling of being alone and separate. There comes a point, when being defined by external criteria, no longer satisfies or fulfills us. What remains is a void that cuts us off from feeling entirely, because it is painful in a way that cannot be consoled, recognized, or mended by anything external.

The acknowledgement of the void inside myself is where my conscious journey started for me, because no sooner had I wondered if there was more, then I had to face what I was honestly feeling in my internal world. It had nothing to do with money or recognition. It had everything to do with feeling happy when I woke up in the morning. How do we know what is more, if we can't define with honesty what is now who we are? The feeling inside myself, as uncomfortable as it was, I knew at some level, was the closest thing there was that could help me understand what might be missing for me. Are you honestly happy with your life, your health, and your relationships? Intuition provides a vehicle to access, that which is deeper than what sits on the surface. It goes beyond the masks we have adopted, the compensations we have made, and the decisions we made that have been long forgotten and yet we are still operating from subconsciously.

Developing our intuitive abilities enables us to first recognize, and then embrace, the potential within an Aspect of Self that seeks liberation. Through intuition, we are led within, to integrate the current Aspect of Self engaged, with the already developed Aspects of Self, to facilitate a fuller experience of who we really are in relation to our Soul, in the physical form. To engage with our intuitive abilities, is to go beyond these specific aspects of personality and expression of who we are as a collective experience, and become united again, with our true Essence, or Soul. When the Aspects of Self are acknowledged in the currently held limitation, we become aware of True Self, the Essence of what we are, that is beyond definition by the intellect. This is Soul. The identities we have come to adopt, such as the mother, the father, the scholar, the philosopher, the artist, are all Aspects of Self, and when subconsciously active, and unrecognized, serve to separate us from who we really are, in our Essence, our original state of Oneness with Divinity. At the level of Essence, with the Aspects in balance, and working in harmony with this Divinity within, we are in Essence, Selfless.

Intuition brings the responsibility for our reality back to us. We can't change our world if we ourselves cannot embrace change. The same world appears differently to each of us because we each see it through our own unique perceptions. Do you see a world filled with hope and unrealized potential? Or do you see a world, where there is nothing you can do, and we are all headed for destruction? Intuition takes us beyond what we think we know, through the place of knowing nothing, to truth, as it exists within us. When we embrace our current truth in honesty, we can move beyond the illusion of what we are, to a greater truth. Intuition is a gift, but more importantly, it is probably the most tangible tool that every living being has access to, naturally. It can serve as the easiest and fastest way to get past what we have become, as we think we are, to a greater experience, one in which we find joy and peace at the level of our Soul, our Essence. To develop intuition requires honesty, and a desire to be free to be who you really are, whatever that may be, naturally.

The teacher is ultimately within. There are those that can help us develop our ability to work with our natural skills, and become reacquainted with them, but it is a personal journey, guided by something so much greater, than what we have come to know as ourselves. The ideas that I am going to share with you have come from my own journey. There have been people and circumstances in my life that have fueled, facilitated, and at times pushed me beyond my comfort level. The further I was pushed by life circumstance, the stronger the desire to find that something more, to fill that feeling of void inside me became, because what I was experiencing, wasn't fulfilling or satisfying me. I simply didn't feel happy. There was nothing wrong in my life; there was just no passion for living. If it had not been for the angels in ordinary clothes that appeared in my life, I would not have learned to embrace the journey within, with joy, and playfulness. The first choice I remember making, was to trust myself, and my inner senses, because I knew they would protect, and guide me. Rather than being tormented by what I couldn't see, or validate from outside sources, I had to go deeper within myself, to find answers. I could be tormented, or I could develop the aspects of myself that facilitated growth and Wholeness. Feeling powerless to change the suffering around me, and trying to make choices, when none seemed right, was not only frustrating, but seemed futile. There had to be another way and I started seeking to find it. There didn't seem to be anyone in my current life that could even relate to what I was seeking, as I was at a loss to define it to them. I was on my own with how I felt. Working with my intuition, or the psychic aspects of myself, proved to guide me out of the unconscious perceptions that no longer served me in the present. By intuitively engaging, we become present in awareness, and by doing so, we learn to recognize the aspect of Self that is actively engaged that has gone unrecognized. These Aspects of Self, when engaged by circumstance, are blind spots to the conscious mind, unless we are able to feel again. Through recognizing our feelings we bring consciousness, through insight, to the part of Self that seeks liberation, and healing.

    The understanding of Self, initially relies on what collectively we have come to acknowledge as the identifiable expressions of who we are, in relation to everyone else. The call from within, is a deeper yearning, from the Soul. To hear our Soul, we have all the Aspects of Self to contend with, because we have unknowingly come to believe, they are who we are. These unconscious Aspects of Self, when not recognized, have the potential to keep us separate from our True Essence, Soul. For many, this feeling of isolation, this not being satisfied with what we have, or not feeling joy in our current experience, this feeling of something missing, is a big void that we are at a loss to define, in any other way than to know, it is a feeling inside that feels impoverished. Interestingly, that inner void, when filled through discovering the Essence of ourselves again, our Soul, naturally manifests external physical representations, that support our Wholeness. We attract energetically and physically all that supports, and nurtures the experience of Soul. In reconnecting with Soul, we are awakened to the illusion that societies collective perceptions have provided for us. The illusion that to be worthy, we must be recognized by societies standards of success, is revealed in truth to be, in acknowledging our own worth, we become examples that set the standards of success, recognized by society. Worthiness and money have become confused with personal value somewhere along the line for many.

The knowledge of Oneness remains in conceptual form for most of us, until we come to *experience* it again. Through the process of integration we become reunited with our innate wisdom, and begin to weave it into the Aspects of Self, that we have developed so far in our life. Since the experience of Oneness originates in the subtle energies, touched first by the subtle senses, then realized through the five physical senses, it is impossible to learn or remember through physical means alone. Just as energy manifests into matter, the process of *becoming* all that we are as Souls, in the human form, comes into being manifest the same way. The seed of potential for each Soul, is in an energetic form, and carries within it the knowledge to sense when the conditions are right for its actualization, through the physical vessel. Nature shows this very concept physically in all living things. The seeds of different plant species, can be put in the ground at the same time, watered and given the same external conditions of light and warmth. Each particular variety will begin to grow at different rates and times. There is an innate knowledge in that particular variety of seed that knows exactly when the conditions are perfect for it to grow and mature. We can force growth, but *thriving* requires honoring the natural rhythms and conditions required to maintain harmony with nature, as nature is required to sustain life.

To *learn* the language of Oneness, can only point us in the direction of actualization, for the process of Self-actualization is an experiential journey that develops a deeper understanding of our existence. The journey of becoming Whole goes beyond words, and explanation in physical terms, as it is experiential. A reason for seeking more in ourselves is often presented when we face a challenge that is beyond our ability to comprehend, accept or live with as we are currently experiencing it. It is through personal experience that we come to appreciate the meaning, in words and descriptions offered by others, who have walked before us in understanding. To work with intuition is to go beyond what we have come to believe about ourselves in relation to our life and relationships, to a deeper truth that we have forgotten, but has always been with us. I believe we all have these innate abilities of greater perception, but we need viable ways in which to access, and learn to work with them again. They are the most natural of our abilities, and yet we have come to doubt them, because of all the other beliefs we have allowed to dictate, and validate how we experience ourselves.

As I began to honor my own intuitive perceptions, my surroundings started to mirror, what my internal world was revealing to me. I began to hear and see validation for what I perceived intuitively. It sometimes was difficult to define what I perceived, as there was no reference already in place that I recognized. It was through observation, rather than immersion, of what was outside myself, that the internal and external experience, started to find clarity. One of my children would answer me out loud when the question had just been in my head. When I would ask why they just said that, they answered because I had just asked. Of course to them my question was odd, because to them, it was as if they had heard me speak it. I actually came to realize, that for most children, these skills, these abilities, are natural to them, and that my questioning seemed ridiculous to them. They had never stopped to think how they knew things; they just naturally operated with these extra senses, assuming it was normal. I think they honestly thought I had lost my mind when I attempted to depict my observations. The validation that I thought I would somehow get from an external source ultimately came from inside me, through this process of discovery. Once we begin consciously seeing beyond what we always believed our world to be, there is validation for our journey everywhere. More importantly, the joy in life is revealed, because this is our natural state regardless of circumstance. The magic in every moment is always there, but to be in tune with subtle energies reveals it more clearly. Being present with the magic, becomes an exercise in common sense, when the simplicity of life, and the synchronicity of events, is revealed through focused awareness, in the moment.

It was becoming aware of the void inside myself that pushed me to seek more. More of what, I had no idea, but it had to be better than the way I currently felt about myself. My life was turned upside down just two years previous to my acknowledgement that I was empty. More importantly, as I have come to realize since, this event changed me, and as a result my life as I had known it ceased to exist. It was like having the rug pulled out from under me and I had no reference of experience that could possibly make sense of it for me. I had to grow and expand in order to meet this challenge because no one in my life had any solutions to share with me on this one. My second child, Harrison, was born. Harrison was diagnosed at birth with Craniosynostoses, which is the premature fusion of the cranial sutures.

I remember, holding this newborn up in front of me a few days after he was released from the hospital following all the tests to confirm the diagnosis, all bundled up in his blanket. He looked like a very old man, with eyes that revealed a very old and wise Soul. This was the first time I knew that the Soul was real because I felt it reach out and take hold of me from within him. I knew somewhere inside myself that he was going to be just fine. There was no supporting evidence that could confirm my knowing he was alright as the CT Scans told another story. So began my conflict between what I felt, and what I was being told must be done. I followed what the Cranial Specialists told me because I didn't want to lose my son, which is what I was told would happen if he didn't have the operation. At one year of age they preformed surgery on Harrison's skull to open the sutures so the brain would have room to grow. During his stay at the Hospital for Sick Children, where the surgery was done for his skull, they also discovered that he also had Infantile Scoliosis. For that year up until his operation, there were many trips to the hospital, for various tests and observations, because there didn't appear to be anyway to clearly identify, or confirm, either his physical or mental capabilities.

My daughter Kate was two years old when Harrison entered our life. She was healthy and happy and was completely joyful and engaged in all that life brought her. I am so grateful that she was there to remind me, and in turn engage me, in the joy that life holds. Kate kept me in that place of believing that no matter what it seemed life was showing you there was an equal gift to be realized if you looked for it. My experience with Kate had validated my skills as a mother, and taught me to play again. Those first two years with her had brought me confidence and great respect for learning from such a little being. She came from me knowing what she needed, and she would wail until I got it. But once satisfied she was happy and content and very engaged with everything. Whether it was hunger, or needing to be held, she was persistent and would let nothing get in the way of her getting her needs met on all levels. Kate taught me to listen, and when I heard her correctly, she was happy. There was no fitting her into my way of thinking, because she knew her own way from the first day she arrived.

Harrison, on the other hand, wasn't as easy to understand. He didn't cry or make a fuss over anything. I had to learn to listen in a new way with him. I also learned to worry with Harrison. So, it was Harrison that created a reason to delve with awareness into the world of subtle energy. It was the only way to hear his needs, because he wanted no part of this reality in the usual ways of babies. During the first year of Harrison's life, with the surgery scheduled for when he was strong enough, it was Kate that kept me focused on what was good in our life. Kate is fifteen now, and she still has that spunk and forthrightness that reminds me "that if it doesn't kill you it will make you stronger." She is a practical Soul that refuses to enter the drama of life as it has a way of being delivered sometimes. So, back then when Kate and Harrison were little, I kept myself focused on realizing the gift and didn't give up until I could find it. It was the only way I was willing to accept any of it. And so it was with Harrison.

If it had not been for Harrison's Soul showing itself so clearly to me as I held him as a baby, I would not have sought within myself, a way to communicate with him. Little did I know at that time, that his birth marked a birth of my own. To hold true to what I knew of Harrison was very difficult in the face of the Medical Community. Harrison had lost his involvement in life following the operation. He was like an empty vessel with the spark of life invisible. His eyes stared straight ahead, and there was no emotion or expression in his eyes, or on his face. The external world was lost to him. He was a fourteen month old, that couldn't walk, talk, communicate, or even want to be engaged or aware of anything around him. He was like a blank page that someone had erased all memory of life from. All I could do was to carry him around with me to try and make him feel safe again. The Medical Doctors all felt the operation was successful, and that possibly further tests, would reveal his mental development more accurately.

I lost myself in the process of trying to find Harrison. I also lost my faith in the Medical Community, because they failed to recognize, that there was something terribly wrong, following the operation. On the surface he physically healed beautifully, but the inside was locked up so tightly there was no reaching him. They hadn't experienced Harrison's brilliance as I had beforehand. They constantly sought to find what was wrong with him, and the answer was always just around the corner with another specialist and test. No answers ever came and I got tired of seeking. We were spending our days waiting to see Specialists at the hospital instead of living. Family and friends felt badly and sorry for us all, and it became very awkward to be around people outside our home. Everyone was trying to make us feel better, but they worried and had little to offer in advice. I suppose just like myself, they figured it was beyond our control, and that we all had to see what would happen, and do our best in the circumstance.

To keep my family on track, and in an attempt to make the best of things, I buried a lot of myself in the process, without even realizing it. So came the time I couldn't live with the situation any longer. I was feeling more and more unhappy, and I had this feeling there was something I was supposed to be doing, but I didn't know what! I had become so attached to Harrison that I couldn't remember ever being away from him. No one around me could help me to see where I had gone off the track, as we were all enmeshed in it. I really felt I had to go somewhere before I lost all sense of reality. At that time I didn't realize the sorrow I had locked up inside myself. I had been operating on automatic to keep going and could not live with myself that way any longer.

When I thought I could contain it no longer, I borrowed money from my mother to go to Peru. It was a planned trip with a group that was going to live with a Shaman for two weeks in the jungle. I didn't really know what the trip was about, except that I knew that I was holding onto so much emotion, that to go somewhere very far and remote with people I didn't know, would be a safe place to deal with whatever came up. The feelings that were becoming harder and harder to contain, could find a way out, that wouldn't hurt anybody. In my mind, I thought that in the jungle, the trees and nature would surely absorb any horrible display of emotion that I might have, if I relinquished control over them. I hadn't studied Shamanism or the rituals of Ayahuasca. For that matter, I had missed the orientation meeting, so I didn't actually know about that part of it at all. I just knew I had to go. Basically, I went on a trip with no idea of what to expect, except that some part of me knew for certain, that I needed it. I did know, that I needed to find myself again, and I went to Peru with this objective. I remember, as the group shared with one another their reason for coming, out of my mouth came the words, "I need to remember who I am. I've forgotten over the past few years." That trip to Peru did change my life, but not for any other reason than it changed me. I came to be clear with my True Self again. I had so much grief and pain stored up that it was keeping me distanced from what could help me the most, my True Self. In those two weeks, I changed, and my life would never look the same to me again. I regained sight of the hopeful world that offered endless possibilities for us all.

I came home knowing that my life was not already decided and laid out for me to just walk through. I had knowingly lived with the vision of having this child attached to my hip for the rest of my life, and unknowingly made his needs be my priority, at the cost of any real happiness for myself. That vision hadn't served any of us at all, least of all Harrison. Letting go of this sense of responsibility, opened the door for some amazing people to enter our life, who helped in ways that I couldn't. Teachers and facilitators became part of Harrison's life, and he was integrated into situations that would help open him to the experience of being alive again. These people believed in him and would help him experience success in becoming a healthy vibrant child again.

I came home to realize that Harrison didn't happen to me, he was the arrival of a great reminder. Any obstacles that I had perceived were only within me. I could do anything I wanted with my life. I didn't know how, but I knew anything was possible. I felt optimistic and encouraged by what surrounded me, not overwhelmed by it. I came home feeling big enough to live my life, and navigate through my challenges, with clarity and faith in a good outcome for us all again. I returned to school to study Traditional Chinese Medicine. I had learned Qigong while away and I loved it. I didn't know what Qi was, or anything about the philosophy, or approach of the discipline of Qigong, so I thought a foundation in Traditional Chinese Medicine would surely teach me what I needed to understand about the eastern approach to physiology, and Qi's part in health. I was interested to find out about Qi, and what was understood about it. I remained devoted to my practice of Qigong. Every morning, before the children got up, I would do half an hour of Qigong. Every evening, after they went to bed, I would do half an hour of Qigong. I began to meditate. I didn't have to go anywhere, it didn't cost anything and it made me feel happy. My energy was constant during the day, and my threshold for what I could handle went way up. I actually started to feel that life wasn't bigger than me. I believed that I could not only do anything I set my mind to, but it would happen naturally one step at a time. I didn't have to have it all figured out before heading out in the direction that felt right. All I had to do, was start trusting myself, and make decisions that felt right for me. I knew in my heart, that my children would benefit as long as I was true to myself.

 I came home with a part of my Self again that I had left behind with the birth of Harrison, and with that missing part came an authentic optimism in what my life held for me at a deeper level. My children survived without me while I was away, and I knew the best thing I could do for them, was to be true to my Self. We couldn't make Harrison different, but we could focus on his potential, rather than his deficiencies. I didn't invest in the outcome with him anymore. This was a very liberating feeling. I just believed in him. Maybe he would come to believe in his abilities to overcome challenge, if we held that example for him. It meant getting on with my life! For some this may seem really selfish, but from what I have since come to understand about trust, this is the greatest demonstration of my faith in him, in his own abilities, that I could show him. To make myself less, in hopes of helping him to feel better about himself, is to demonstrate limitations and my lack of faith in him. I also stopped worrying about Harrison, because I realized every worry I had, was information I was sending to him energetically, to confirm my lack of faith in his abilities to meet his challenges. Worrying was not going to boost Harrison's self esteem, on any level; it would only enforce his self-doubts about his ability to overcome challenge.

I truly believe in Harrison, and at some level he is making choices every day for how he wants to see and experience himself. If I help him be reliant, and compensate with everything that appears to me to be missing within him, how will he come to realize what he needs? There have been physical needs that he has required assistance with over the years, but even these he has learned to do for himself now. There is not a thing we can do to help him if he doesn't come to realize his own needs. The irony is this; when Harrison was born I hadn't yet realized myself what needs I had, as a woman. Not until I became so run down, and lost in my role as mother, did I begin to hear that call from within, trying to get my attention. There had to be more…

My journey with Harrison has been very rich in experience for us both. It was like stepping back in time with him, to the stage when infants become toddlers. The desire that naturally emerges in a baby, to obtain what is just out of reach to them, needed rekindling in Harrison. The natural process spurred by curiosity that a baby has to explore an object just out of reach and their exploration of various tactics to get you to get it for them is how they develop the skills to go after it themselves when you fail to retrieve it. Learning to crawl, learning to talk, learning to get their needs recognized so they can get what they want are all products of desire. With a child with special needs it is a constant reassessment as to what is a "will not" and what is a "can not."

When I look back at this now, I can't imagine how I could have lived without realizing the role that intuition had in guiding me. That void that I felt, was a deep yearning to reconnect with my Soul, but I didn't understand what was calling me. It was my Soul trying to reach me through my pain, to remind me who I am, but I didn't recognize it. The frustration I had experienced before going to Peru, this sense of urgency within me, was my inability to recognize my intuition, as a true need for me to acknowledge. Even though my intuition has shown itself to me for as long as I can remember, to live in its acknowledgement, has brought great liberation to the way I feel about trusting my choices, and experience of today. Those events that pull the rug out from under our feet are the biggest blessings heaven could send our way. For me, this is what it took to shake me up enough, to wake up, and realize what I was doing with my life, and my abilities.

What you find in the following pages are the places that Spirit has taken me. My children, Kate, Harrison and Alex and my life partner Mikhael have been my greatest teachers. They have grounded me, they have loved me, and they have shown me that working with energy is simple and authentic and it always leads to the truth. This material is my own synthesis of what has come on the wings of Spirit to be part of me, and for that, every aspect of life must be acknowledged. By quieting the mind and learning to listen with the heart my journey has not only revealed that there is so much more than what we currently are able to experience of ourselves but also in every other living thing. There is magnificence expressed through the very life force in all of us.

I don't believe that anything in this world is actually original, rather I believe everything in this world carries a part of the Origin. How we each take this knowledge and integrate it with our own experience becomes our individuality, but there are common truths we all recognize within ourselves at the level of our Soul. This to me is the celebration of diversity and unity that has been referred to as the experience of Wholeness and oneness by many cultures and philosophies. The diversity being the realization of our individual expressions of Self, which leads us to the experience of Wholeness, and the unity being the realization of the common truths of our Soul, which leads us to the celebration of Oneness. May we become inspired to find faith in True Self again, learn to trust our intuition as the teacher within, and summon the courage to be who we are, present in our life, and with all those we allow to touch us, and in turn be touched by us. It is in opening ourselves with honesty, that we are released from the cage of illusion that our current perceptions have created for us, in this moment.

BELIEVE IN YOURSELF

*Somewhere inside yourself
listen to that voice that tells you, I can do this!*

Even if it is just a whisper, mixed with some self-doubt that wonders if maybe you are different and special in some way. Maybe it feels like a figment of your imagination that gave you the idea or dream of being something really incredible! As a child do you remember having this feeling that you were going to do something really, really important with your life? When you grew up they would all see how amazing you are and be sorry that they hadn't taken you seriously just because your body was small and you couldn't explain everything you knew to be true.

Would you suspend your apprehensions for just a short time to entertain the possibility that you could be so special that others would come to experience you in that way as well? What do you have to lose? Unless of course, you are completely happy in all aspects of yourself and your life, which means that health, wealth and prosperity on all fronts is now your current experience. Working with people's health, and a desire to uncover the truth of their state of disease within them has brought such inklings to the surface on more than one occasion in my office. It seems that the knowledge of being special is inside each of us, we just don't believe it anymore from what our current perceptions are mirroring to us.

We are all special, unique and beautiful beings. This is our natural state, even if it is buried so deeply we don't remember it any longer. For many, it is buried under many layers of how we have come to experience ourselves, and come to believe ourselves to be, through our life circumstance. Whatever happened to that spunky kid that thought they had the world by the tail? Something happened, or a series of things happened that got in the way. Everything that happened before this moment is in the past, but you can choose to start this minute to unveil the truth of who you are. There are a few deceptions, illusions, compensations, and things that we have taken on without realizing it, but none of them has power over our true nature, unless we allow them to dictate and direct us unknowingly.

I don't think anyone chooses to lie to themselves purposely. I also don't think that we always deceive others intentionally, unless we are unknowingly threatened in some way. In other words, self-deception is possibly the unconscious compensation we adopt, when we feel self-preservation is at risk. In line with our true nature, I believe we are all good people with good intentions, but let's face it; many are not functioning in awareness of their true nature. When we do lie, or show deception, there usually lies hidden within us a fear of having our vulnerability exposed, and therefore the belief that the initial experience of betrayal will be repeated. We make decisions about how we will respond in the present, by assumptions about others, based on our experience in similar situations, in the past. These decisions and thoughts of ourselves, that have a negative emotional charge, were made at a time to preserve ourselves in a particular circumstance, but over time we forget ever having made them. These beliefs about ourselves, or our life, become our adopted way of operating, and it works for a while until we reach a point where it no longer serves us, and we can't figure out what we're doing that is keeping us from moving forward in a better experience. We rewrite the past, to help justify the present, in an attempt to keep our personal lies, and deceptions in tact. We also look to blame everything around, and outside of ourselves, to keep from facing the fact, that we may have to change. It can only be something or someone else's fault for so long... until we exhaust all possibilities that implicate another for our own repeated experience of inadequacy, or discomfort.

So, what if we were to fully embrace faith in ourselves, to reveal that which no longer serves us in the present? We need to look within ourselves to find these answers. A decision can be changed if we can come to recognize having made it in the first place. The starting place I have identified is to start believing in yourself again and your natural ability to find truth within yourself. To consciously choose to be honest with yourself, about the way you feel, is to begin to strengthen your internal resources that can reveal clarity.

BE OPEN TO THE POSSIBILITY THERE MAY BE MORE

*Getting beyond our personal experience
and current knowledge of our Self and life.*

There is always something to learn in every situation. You may surprise yourself with what else is being revealed if you entertain the possibility there may be more. Even the greatest joys in our life can reveal new understanding to our perceptions. For every negative there is an equal positive. If you are currently only seeing one polarity of the experience there is more to be revealed. To see things the way they really are is to gain perspective of the whole spectrum of experience, including both polarities. Intuition is a viable way to become observer of what is being shown in its truth, not just our interpretation, or personal relationship to it. To be in the place of consciously choosing how you wish to experience life is to take responsibility for your experience. To take responsibility for our Self and our perceptions is to be committed to healing. Not just healing on the physical level but on the emotional, mental and spiritual levels as well.

Let's take the example of feeling upset, or meeting resistance in a current life situation. That's easy for most of us on a daily basis. This discomfort surfaces when with another person, or we find ourselves in a circumstance that leaves us feeling uncomfortable. We first tend to look at the situation for what is being done to us that would cause such pain. We can come up with several reasons *why* this person or that person would want to hurt us, or take something from us. Do these possible reasons serve any purpose but to justify our own viewpoint, as we would like to hold onto it? After all, these reasons keep us believing it is another that has the problem, or that they are the ones that need to change, not us. But to ask *what* is the feeling of upset, resistance, or discomfort, is to take what appears to exist externally as the problem, to a reference that represents an internal limited perception or belief about our Self, in that situation. The internal perception being the way we are experiencing what is happening, subconsciously, with an Aspect of our Self in that moment. *What* does it feel like to us, personally, in that moment? This is closer to the truth and gives us a reference that can take us back to the root cause of the original feeling. The feeling of being upset is a trigger for a Sensitivity we have encapsulated inside, from the past. Once the emotional charge is removed from the causal level, not from the current experience, we have the ability to see our part in it, as we really are. If we can change our viewpoint to one that is objective, and no longer personal, we have the ability to become observer of the original experience in its truth, then healing follows naturally because there is nothing standing in the way of us realizing it. If we can use intuitive tools to help heal the original trauma or negative experience and come to the realization of the gift it gave us, is there anything to resonate with the current situation that causes discomfort? Not anymore... the stuck part of Self has been liberated into a greater understanding. The current situation no longer feels personally about us, because we see it for what it is, that is all. The current situation can be perceived without the filter that protected our Sensitivity getting in the way. We are now free to see the situation in its entirety for what it really is, and who we are in our truth, in the present.

Maybe the situation just becomes a neutral experience, but we see our part in it more clearly and not as the victim of circumstance. Maybe the whole thing isn't just about us personally! Maybe it is about everyone, and depending on what needs to be healed in each person we will all perceive the events completely differently. So, if each takes responsibility for unveiling their part, and where they feel resistance in seeing the situation in its truth, think of the potential of each event to transform into something equally positive for each of the participants. The potential exists in any situation for each of the *participants* to be elevated to a greater experience of themselves. There is a glitch that has probably crossed your mind here, in the scenario I have just described. In a perfect world, where we are all living in awareness, or at least one in each gathering is aware, this becomes a viable possibility. But, in many situations that we experience resistance, rejection, or unwillingness of another to receive our honesty, this is very difficult. Even if they are still sitting in the same room with us, unless they are committed to the process of transforming discord into harmony, it's very difficult for us to find peace with it, with them. Most of us are holding onto perceptions from a long time ago, or even yesterday, that others involved are not present to resolve with us. The Process of Inner Alchemy is not reliant on anyone, except you, being present in honesty. The beauty of working intuitively, with the Process of Inner Alchemy, is the opportunity it gives us to resolve our discomfort, without reliance on any external criteria, including other people. It becomes all about what we internally perceive as our reality that has gone unrecognized by us.

To discover you are truly special can be a wonderful revelation. To be special though, is not to be better than someone else. Only you can be the best you, no one else can emulate, copy, steal, or take what is essentially your individuality or expression of the greater truth of who you are. Your contribution is a unique expression of you. To try and be anything but your True Self is to guarantee failure. How can you not succeed at being yourself? You may stumble, discover some nasty habits and games you have adopted over the years, but ultimately these illusions will be revealed if you believe in yourself. You will be led right back to your infinite potential if you remain honest with yourself. The God within is alive and well, but connecting with it takes some healing of wounds, and illusions of separation, from our Divine Essence. The more we liberate these aspects of ourselves that stand between us and our own Divinity, the more we see the potential in all that surrounds us. As we become real, there we are, face to face, with the GOD question. All of a sudden, reality has shifted, to reveal there is so much more, than we had ever imagined. Opening ourselves to the experience of subtle energy, opens us to the great other dimensions of our being.

AND WHAT ABOUT GOD IS ALL THIS?

To work with intuition is to come to terms with our beliefs about the Divine-restoring faith in something greater than what we currently know of our being.

I'm sure that I'm not the only person in the world that was raised with certain unconscious ideas about what God was or where God was. But I actually never questioned it until I embraced my intuitive abilities on a conscious level. To connect intuitively, is to leap with faith into dimensions of our being, that have no boundaries or limitations for the perceptions, beliefs, or values that we have come to know through our physical reality. It is the unseen power within all living things. The sacred teachings, such as the *Hermetica*, tell us of an unseen but omnipresent power, but to experience it is another thing all together. To know the experience of God is different than to know about God. I used to hear the word, God, and automatically dismiss what I was experiencing of love. Somewhere, locked inside me, was a belief that I wouldn't have experienced trauma or suffering if God really loved me. I didn't even recognize that I had this belief, but up it came when I opened the door to question what God was. When I work with others intuitively, God is there with me as part of the process, to guide and illuminate what is being shown to me. Now, if I said, when I work intuitively, Love is there with me as part of the process, to guide and illuminate what is being shown to me, does it become more palatable? I had to make peace with what I was taught to believe and what was presented as reality to me about God. The two seemed to be at complete odds until I resolved it. It became a question that I wasn't exactly sure where the answer would come from, but I was pretty sure; it wasn't going to come from anywhere inside myself. I came to the conclusion that God, which is Love, is ultimately a personal and sacred experience for us to make peace with somewhere along our journey to unveiling our Essence. In unveiling our Essence, we come to know and appreciate that we are Love. So, the words I have read hundreds of times over about God, that I couldn't relate to, have really been about what I had yet to discover and relate to harmoniously, within myself, Love.

This is how it happened for me. Embracing the sacredness of the Divine happened for me in my kitchen. This is not a surprise, as the most illuminating and miraculous events have always happened in the most ordinary of places for me. One morning, while I was making breakfast, I had a dialogue running in my head that was wondering exactly what God was. I was pondering the possibilities of what God was exactly and if indeed it was a One Force type of thing, or more like a Master Mind. As I was preparing the food, and being with my thoughts in my head, another dialogue interrupted my thoughts, and was quite anxious to be heard. Until that moment I believed my pondering was a personal thought process. When this presence arrived on the scene and it was apparent that the dialogue was not private, I was a bit overwhelmed and I felt angry. After all these were very personal thoughts… in my private internal world! I felt completely exposed with nowhere to hide. It hadn't occurred to me that it could actually be God in dialogue with me. I stood there and listened. It was as if the "me," as I knew myself, that had been talking in my head became the observer, and the dialogue was between someone really angry inside me, and this great presence that was above me. I realize this sounds odd, but this is the best way I can describe it. It wasn't a fight, as the presence wasn't angry. It was very calm and considerate.

I was witnessing an interaction between this presence right above me and some angry voice inside me that I didn't recognize. It was an energy that was presenting itself to a part of me that was deep in my belly. There was no form, nothing I could define except a very real presence. I stood there in my kitchen, attending with every ounce of my being, to this very big and impressive presence. I felt like an animal caught in the car headlights, frozen, in disbelief. It was at a point in my journey when I was trying to work through understanding my own extrasensory perceptions and how to navigate functioning in my life with what felt like one foot in another reality. Quite frankly, if this presence had decided to take me out with its breath, that would have been fine with me, because I was struggling hard with what my intuition was revealing to me about myself, and the fear of the unknown, where I was being led. I decided to surrender to what was happening because I honestly didn't feel in any danger, as I stood in my kitchen, and felt nothing but good could ultimately come of it. It didn't really seem an option to avoid this anyway. When the voice inside me became quiet and calm, I found myself in direct dialogue with this presence. I was told that I could call it anything I wanted. Heavenly Mother, God, Goddess, The Divine, Great Spirit, absolutely anything I liked. The possibilities were emerging, and I really tried on a few things to see what would happen. Trying them on, led to, *I am* Heavenly Mother, I am Kuan Yin, and I am Divine. I tried them all but couldn't quite embrace the idea that I could be God. I was laughing and talking out loud at this point. And to think I wondered about people walking down the street talking to themselves. Maybe they had known something I didn't all along.

Then came an inspiration. What if God was a name that represented something that was greater than us all but wasn't separate from us, just more than each separate expression? I wondered if redefining the name of God might help. What did God mean? **G**reat **O**ther **D**imension seemed to allow me to break free from the beliefs and ideas I had been raised with. It evoked a different understanding that still needed exploration, but was more than I had previously believed. It opened the door to something "more" than I had accepted in my current experience. I liked it because this energy was actually something that could be felt and understood yet not of this world as I knew it exactly. It seemed to come in response to that something "more" that I had been seeking. The presence that had been above me felt like it came in to me and united with that voice that was coming from my belly. I felt full and heavy but peaceful. The "more" I was seeking turned out to be within me all along. My previously held belief in God was what separated me from receiving it in its fullness. I couldn't see God, but it was definitely real in every other sense of it. It wasn't male or female but God seemed to be a masculine name. So what would Goddess be? **G**reat **O**ther **D**imensions with an 'ess'. Now I liked that even better especially in reference to the feminine energies of intuition. The feminine feels more encompassing like a force that gently embraces and seems soft and expansive in its presence. The feminine energy seemed to be multi-dimensional in its very nature. The masculine energy, more focused, directed and can be targeted very specifically with focused intent. Neither of these seem to fit the presence of God as I experienced it though– as it honestly didn't feel male or female, it was just big and I knew it was trying to help me understand and accept it. It felt alive and all encompassing, so "it" doesn't really do justice.

Now, I could accept that I had Great Other Dimensions as a being, because all the parts of myself that were beyond my physical body were real, through awareness of subtle energy. The idea of separation was mine, and over the next few months I came to understand that this Great Other Dimension is in every living thing, including me and it is very magical and approachable and the nicest presence to be with, that I had ever experienced. I felt Love, like I had never experienced it before. There is proof all around us, every minute, every day in all ways, but we have to be reminded how ordinary it is. Extra ordinary really because it is ever present and nothing living is without it! With the intellect, this we all know, but to experience it brings that Greater Other Dimension into our being and experience of self. No description could possibly give God justice, but the experience of the God Energy to me would be similar to meeting the nicest guy in the world.

GOD IS LIKE THE NICEST GUY IN THE WORLD...

that no one takes notice of, unless they need something, and there he would be if you looked for him, but for most, he would be invisible in the crowd. He would be single, asexual, considerate, nothing would be judged right or wrong by him. He would always listen carefully, and offer sincere and truthful feedback when asked, not worrying about what you thought of him. He would be there no matter what, and love you anyways, even if he knew you didn't need to be in pain, but needed to experience feeling separate, for that moment. He would always have his hand stretched out with a welcoming smile, so if you reached through your pain, and the illusion of separation, you would find him patiently holding the light for you to step into, and embrace. He would be faithful to your highest potential, and encourage you to seek it. If you fell he'd be the first to give you a hand up, show you the humor of your ways, and tell you to go try again another way. He would always be there, but most of the time when things were going great, you'd forget to acknowledge him. He gets taken for granted a lot, but doesn't seem to hold a grudge about it… because he is the nicest guy in the world and everyone knows, and loves him, even if its just because they have heard of him, and not personally acknowledged or accepted his presence yet.

To embrace our intuition is to once again be united with the Greater Other Dimensions of our being. An aspect of Self becomes recognized as an opportunity to liberate True Self, and we begin to experience Soul, in its truth. Soul unveiled, has the ability to transcend any preconditioned ideas of who we think we are, that has separated us from experiencing the Love in ourselves, the Love in others, and the Love in all life.

KNOW NOTHING

Be honored to sit in the place of knowing nothing,
open to receive information and knowledge beyond the physical senses.

After finding myself in personal relationship with God, this one was pretty easy for me. No one needed to remind me that I knew nothing, because from that moment on I felt like I was seeing everything for the first time. To intuitively receive information, the part of us that thinks it knows what something is about, has to step aside. In allowing ourselves to be guided by energy we take what is presented in the moment, tune into it and receive information from what it expresses on the subtle energy level, either in sound, the way it feels, an emotion, a smell, a body sensation, or just a knowing. It is to sit in the place of knowing nothing in order to receive what is being sensed in its truth, not our interpretation, based on our own thoughts or experience. There are many ways in which intuitive information can be received, but the more humility and genuine attending we are able to do, the more accurate the information. To be a Medical Intuitive, is to go beyond what is presented by a diagnosis, to understand what the individual's body is actually expressing through its energy, or the energy around it, about its state of disease. Intuition is not limited to being Medically based, just as our fine motor skills of writing are not limited to one application. To engage our intuitive abilities in general terms, is to bring expanded awareness into the present moment. Through engaging our subtle senses, we may be guided to a higher truth that serves to liberate what is beyond the intellect's current perception, and facilitate the realization of the innate potential present, in that moment.

COURAGE

Be courageous enough to start each day as you would the first day of Kindergarten, with the belief that the world is good and pure and that you can do anything, because it is safe to be yourself.

With Sensitivity to our intuition cultivated, imagination and creativity become natural expressions of our true self. Many of us can't remember that first day of Kindergarten, and some of us do, because it wasn't a good experience. But pretend you had a great childhood and entering school was an adventure. Kindergarten was an opportunity to explore and engage with others just like you. You had great ideas already about yourself, and weren't afraid to try new things. But what you thought about many things, was in that moment anyway, because you hadn't yet gotten attached to being right all the time. There was no need to defend what you thought was right, because your past was not coloring your perceptions of the present, as it really existed without prejudice. Everyone can be right in his or her own way in Kindergarten. You learned about other people, and new ways to do things, and at the end of the day you came home with something more than you left with that morning. Learning to be considerate of other people, and their needs, is also part of this time. Off to school to play, and it never occurred to you to place expectations for achievement on yourself, or consider there were any obstacles to get in your way. You assumed that everything you ever imagined was possible, because nothing in your experience had shown you otherwise. Reconnecting with your intuitive abilities is like having the opportunity to begin Kindergarten again with the intent to be yourself, being playful and forgiving of mistakes and open to what this beautiful life in all its color and expressions has to show you.

To intuitively receive information is to become the observer. It is like being in Heaven reporting what subtle energy, reveals about a current situation on earth, whether it is physically, mentally or spiritually based. There is personal detachment to the process as it is reporting, and communicating between subtle energy forms and the physical reality. It is like being Heaven on Earth in service to help mankind with our health, our relationships, our understanding of the life experience as Soul, within the human vessel. The Great Other Dimensions of our being are revealed through intuitively perceiving. Perspectives and perceptions are all relative.

PART TWO:

Embracing a New Perspective

When we become tuned into the Feminine Energy of Intuition, we consciously embark on a journey that we thought was 'not real' up to that point, because we had no way to relate to it, with certainty. Those *Great Other Dimensions* become tangibly experienced as our *reality* because we can now tangibly feel, touch, and know them with our subtle senses. We in turn, become real ourselves, in a way that is hard to imagine is possible. Intuition can ultimately take us past Self, to the depths of our being, where we meet the perspective of Soul.

IMAGINE FOR A MOMENT...

that we are in heaven before coming to earth. We are having a meeting with all the Souls discussing what we see happening on earth. We know who we are, and there is unconditional love for Self and all the other Souls. We are in full knowledge of our being, and are watching what is happening down below us in disbelief. We can't believe that our fellow Souls are acting and living the way they are, in complete contradiction to what they know to be true of themselves. We are moved to want to go and remind them, so they can enjoy earth as a beautiful paradise in which to experience themselves.

Then, our Soul is cautioned. " It is very hard to remember once you have been exposed to the human condition for any length of time. You will begin to doubt yourself. You will begin to experience some of the negative emotions, and are going to be swayed by them. Are you secure enough in what you know of the light, to stand true to what you know in the face of adversity?" As a Soul in full realization in heaven, we are absolutely sure we will remember the pureness and goodness of who we are.

So, the earth experience is explained in great detail. " Earth is the garden of paradise. It is full of reminders of who you really are. The trees, rocks, and animals are all one with you. Everywhere you look you will find your likeness. The natural elements are reminders to help you stay true to yourself."

"Imagine it is an elaborate play called Love, and you are going to be given a special part. No one else can be cast in this particular aspect of Love. Only you can be that part- so the play depends on you being true to your true nature. This is an ongoing play and the players are all intricately staged. All you have to do is show up, and BE who you are, and the orchestration will be taken care of by heaven above."

"In being true to your Self, you will help awaken others to remember this within themselves. It is like a light going on. Some will refer to this as Life Purpose. So many in search of their life purpose are looking to satisfy this desire with the trappings of the human condition, because they have forgotten the truth about themselves. They focus on what job should they do, where should they live, and what should be their specific contribution to the world of earth? It is a very difficult task to find one's life purpose. On the other hand, it is very simple to BE it." "To be true to yourself in a situation, is to contribute your individual expression of Love, and as such, you will know what is being called forward to do, from within you. Remember above all else, that it is heaven that orchestrates and brings about the stage that you are to step out onto when you receive your cue. Just keep your heart open to hear the prompt. If you get too caught up in the misconceptions of the human race you will become deaf to that which is calling you."

"You will catch yourself asking, 'What can I give of myself in this situation?' And maybe in remembering your Essence, as you are here in heaven, you will ask 'What of myself am I being called to *bring forward* in this moment, so others will come to know this one part of Love?' In the play of Love on earth, you are but one part of the Whole. Your contribution is but one part of the play! That is all. The experience of Wholeness relies on the various Souls parts being present in the play. In being your part, truly, deeply and passionately, others will be given the opportunity to bring forward their part."

This is where Heaven's orchestration is truly Divine because no one in the moment really knows how it all fits together. Your part in that moment may not seem perfect, or feel perfect, or sound perfect, but it will be authentically an expression of you in that moment. Others then are moved to bring forward who they are in response to you. It may not be a good experience all of the time, but it evokes honesty and integrity in the Essence of the play. When everyone focuses on what they bring of themselves, and summon the courage to just being a 'part', the doors open to unveil the truth of our Wholeness. There is nothing to lose of yourself, except the risk of exposing your humanness. There is much to gain, in having faith that your single act carries the potential of bringing yourself closer, to the experience of Wholeness. In this simple act of coming forward, with who you are in the present, you are aligning with a greater knowledge of yourself and others, and the opportunity is born to take one step closer to playing in your full presence. If earth is paradise, then it should be joyous and fun.

Each player has everything they need at any given moment, whether they realize it or not. From the vantage point of heaven, it is easy to see that there is nothing that we can give another that they don't already have within them, in their Essence. A reminder is all we can be to one another. If they don't already know it, how will they become aware of that void they are experiencing, if we keep filling it in with illusion for them? In *giving* them something of ourselves, other than our full presence, we are further feeding the illusion of mankind. This is where our separateness stems from. Instead of being our part, we keep ourselves in the experience of being apart. And besides, are we really being true to our Soul, if we believe we fundamentally have more than someone else? We are each Love, and together we are the many expressions and fullness of Love. It is through the experience of our Soul, in awareness that we have the potential, to be all expressions of Love.

We are each unique. We each shine in different ways. As a society we have created many diversions to fill that void of not experiencing our brilliance. Or more to the point, we have conveniently adopted accepted means to spend our time, energy and resources. We have lots of toys, lots of products, lots of manufactured food, lots of entertainment, lots of whatever you can think of.... except that any one of these in excess has the potential to bring us closer to that experience of emptiness. There is no life value to them, except that which we place with them. We are life. Life, no matter how advanced our intellect becomes, cannot be manufactured, it is created. These *things* are mere expressions of us, so if we forget who we are, they too carry that energy of emptiness with them.

If we believe that we can *give* another something that they don't have within themselves, then possibly this is a reflection of our own separation from a higher truth. The physical expressions of our world are things that belong with us for a while. These are not actually ours to give, but merely to use and pass on in the support of our experience. If we stay clear in what our Soul knows, then another will come to experience a greater truth within them, and the physical manifestations around us all will reflect that truth. It is within us, and only we can connect to it. Others may touch it, others may know it, but only individuals can be and express it perfectly for themselves. As we each realize more of our truer potential, we all benefit on an energetic and physical level. The Source of us all becomes richer from our individual experiences.

When others fail to step forward we need to be prepared to stand clearly in our light, alone for a time, with a hand outstretched until they remember to trust and have faith again. Stage fright can take over for many, but it becomes much easier to step out into the bright light when there are others already on stage showing us there is nothing to be afraid of. The stage in its illusion of exposing our Sensitivities, can seem a greater threat than it actually has the capability of being. In relinquishing our control over how we will be received, and placing our focus on what we bring forward from our heart, the illusion is exposed. It is this very act of taking that one step forward that reveals the path our heart knows to follow.

When we hear the faint whispers of nature reminding us, step forward with courage to listen. All we have to be is our Self at that moment. With courage be truly, and passionately our Self. Life purpose will be revealed through the act of each step we take, being true to our Self. Being true to our Self, is when we come forward, with what we honestly think and feel about something in our heart. This becomes our steps in the direction of Soul. From the vantage point of heaven, looking down and not having an emotional investment in this process, it seems very simple. But for those who have been living in the midst of the human condition for any length of time there is much that stands between the way they see and experience and the larger picture. We become programmed with beliefs and values that serve staying where we are, to fit in the environment we are conditioned to. Sometimes when it's our turn to come forward, with our part in the earth play, or to speak our truth in the face of adversity, we forget the importance, and hang out backstage waiting for a better opportunity, or signal that it's our turn. It doesn't feel safe to expose our dissatisfaction, or hurts, because it is a threat to our security and acceptance by others. In that moment to be silent feels safe, but in reality, we are paving the road to keeping ourselves at the mercy of others decisions, and isolated in our experience. Life will continue to be perceived as happening to us, instead of us realizing our part in awareness, and becoming active in our choices. By remaining passive in our experience, we are in reality allowing things to remain the same in our perception of their limitations, and their power over us is endorsed by the perception of our Self, that is separate from Soul.

Bringing this into relationship with what we can relate to within the context of our life, walking the earth in everyday experience, is where intuition allows us to go past what we think something to be, to see it in its higher truth. When we engage intuitively, we can look past the way things appear, to see what is inherent. When I was recently in the Philippines, I had the privilege of staying at a Convent, The Assumption Sabbath Place, where there was a school of children, being taught by the Nuns. We were up in the mountains in Baguio City, where the Native people have integrated their beliefs with modern civilization. It was the courage of these nuns and children to speak, walk, and demonstrate their beliefs, that I came to see we are not so different after all. The Native children, who attended this school, did a presentation for us, and the message delivered by an eight-year-old girl, was about when the Spaniards came, and mined the gold from the mountains, and left behind the damaged land and mountains. As a united people, although from different Tribes, they realized that the gold could be taken from the land, but that the land could heal if they cared for it, and that the true richness was left untouched in their hearts. She spoke of Oneness with each other and the world. The nuns told us about the philosophy of the school, and that they had placed focus on encouraging the children to embrace, and keep their native ritual and beliefs alive. Christianity, as we know it, was not taught at this school. The presentation they gave, was of their Native dances, and music. As I watched these children, I realized that any poverty we saw in their community was merely a reflection, of our own impoverishment on the spiritual level. Up in the mountains, the natives are still living simply, unmoved in their faith in nature's power, even though there is upheaval of their changing land. I felt so grateful for them sharing their faith, their optimism, their devotion to their families, their land, and their culture, with us. As this young girl narrated the story, everyone there was moved to feel One with those children. In their courage to bring forward who they are, we were moved, to open ourselves to the message of the heart that went beyond words or personal experience. I came home with the realization, that it is quite possibly our third world countries, that we perceive to be so impoverished, that in truth, are the very meaning of richness, the rest of the world so desperately needs reminding of at this time. On opposite ends of the globe we demonstrate to one another the polarities of impoverishment. I am hopeful we will awaken to realize what is our true *richness*, and realize we are not separate, so we may care for another, and share with one another, our developed resources that support fulfilled life, for us all.

IS AN ANIMAL IN CAPTIVITY SAFER THAN IN THE WILD?

The animal in the wild is aware of his environment, and his instincts are keen to navigate in his environment. The animal in captivity is cared for. Which one seems safer to you? Learning to take responsibility for our experience is like being released from captivity into the wilderness, for the first time. It can be an incredible experience, where we become aware of the beauty, freedom and possibility that stand before us, or we can have so many fears of the unknown, that we are frozen outside the cage door, afraid to venture out into the new territory. We have already decided what the unknown holds for us, based on our fears, before we even explore it for what it is. Being in the cage in its limitations has the illusion of safety, but we are completely reliant on others meeting our needs, and deciding when, and how, to care for us. We may not like it all the time, and yet feel powerless to express it, because it could be the end of us.

To become responsible, means to first acknowledge what we currently feel, and what we desire for ourselves. The cage may provide for all our needs beautifully, but chances are the experience of freedom, is what our Soul is calling us toward. Developing our natural skills, like intuition, can empower us, to venture out of the cage door, feeling safe and inspired to investigate the perceived wild, to decide for ourselves, what experience we will have in it. Is it possible that the wilderness is actually truer to home, in its ability to meet our needs, than the cage? Animals born into captivity still have their natural instincts, but they need reminding and support, until they gain confidence in them again, because they have grown up without the experience of using them. To me we are not unlike this animal when we embark on the journey of Self, because it is following instincts and innate knowledge within us, that we are guided to our natural state of freedom.

Our Soul yearns to be free, and yet many have not been raised in an environment that nurtured self-reliance or the concept of individual responsibility. The intuitive abilities have long been relinquished in the process of becoming just like everyone else, because somewhere within us, we believed it would keep us safe, and give us a sense of belonging. Stepping out onto that perceived stage of life, in Essence, is to confront the illusion of separation, created by the cage we have known as home. Unlike animals, as human beings, our cage is an illusion. The cage as home is actually the unknown, because we have no idea as to whether or not our needs will be met, from one moment to the next. We are at the complete mercy of someone, or something outside ourselves acknowledging, and caring for us as long as we fulfill our part, according to their expectations. The cage seems to be the unknown, when we look at it from this vantage point. The wilderness, from this same vantage point, has the qualities we know at a deeper level, the level of the Soul, that are truer to the virtues of home. Home being where we all originally came from, like Heaven. A home like heaven is a safe place to be ourselves, with others that love us, and understand us, and support our need to grow, and explore, and experience our Wholeness. It is important to remember, the more we can maintain clarity of this truth, that it is safe to be ourselves, the more challenging the scenes in our earth experience will be, that we are summoned to come forth in, to transform with our clarity.

The wilderness can seem really scary if it's the first time we've ventured out into it. Humanity has created the illusion, that it is very difficult, or next to impossible to survive there. Just one glimpse from the perspective of heaven exposes this false perception in its truth. Intuition is our means to gain the perspective of heaven, within ourselves. The cage appears safe, when living with limited perceptions, whereas the wilderness appears to be our unrealized potential, when secure in our awareness of who we really are. There is no threat in the wilderness when we trust ourselves. The vitality, the beauty, the reminders of natures power, all become supportive of our experience, as long as we remain true to Self in awareness, and respect of the resources, internally and externally, that support our Wholeness.

BEING HEAVEN ON EARTH

It is only one step away for any of us at anytime.

From the vantage point of Heaven, looking down at it all, it is hard to imagine what could keep so many from just being themselves when their single act of love could transform so much around them. Sometimes honesty doesn't feel like love, and to speak it carelessly can create hurt. Even truth that hurts us, when spoken from the heart, can be transforming because it is out in the open. Others can decide how they wish to respond, rather than pretending to go along with the accepted lie, because it seems more comfortable. Much effort goes into building and sustaining the illusions that start out the most innocent of ways. I believe it all stems from the fear of being hurt or the fear of hurting another. And the irony is, that hurt ultimately becomes the experience of our personal reality, because we betray our true Self and others in the process, and don't remember our part in its inception.

The big picture from above is about a full and magnificent expression of who we are. We are love in its many expressions, not to be judged, but to be experienced by us all, to grow in understanding of our true nature. Not all good, and not all bad. To walk with humanity in awareness, is to stay open to feel and experience the many expressions of this core truth, remembering the oneness that we all were in knowledge of, from Heaven above.

In our openness we step into the reality that all that appears and feels negative, when touched by this simple truth, has the ability to be transformed into an equally positive expression of who we are. Our life purpose becomes clearer, when we begin to remember and experience inside, that we are Love. Every situation, every living thing perceived from this knowingness allows us creative expression, and an ability to hear the call to stand in our truth of this knowledge. In stepping forward, we remind others to trust themselves, and connect with them, at a level that cuts through the illusion of isolation. Every tool, every bit of education, all our life experience, every resource at any given moment, can be called forward and creatively adapted to facilitate that moment. Tapping into our internal resources, brings integrity back to True Self. To be moved by what is internally supported, with kindness and compassion, we are serving our purpose in creating this paradise we have named Earth, to reflect our magnificence. Learning to hear our Soul and the Soul of one another requires remembering how to listen with the heart. Intuition is about using the subtle senses to listen to a more expansive, more dimensional expression of our being. Sensing Intuitively creates a bridge, between our current perceptions, and the perceptions held subconsciously by the body, that create disease within us.

DISEASE IS A SYMPTOM

A symptom expresses a deeper discomfort with our Being.

Disease is the manifestation of the discomfort our body is trying to communicate to us in the only way it knows we will come to recognize it, through a symptom. Medical Intuition specifically, is about using the extra senses to identify the imbalances, the truer state of dis-ease that the physical, emotional, spiritual, and mental bodies are expressing, as it relates to the state of health of the individual. The body is the expert for the individual's disease, not the Intuitive. The intuitive is the observer and recorder because the Intuitive can discern the language of the body, mind and Spirit of the individual. Intuition itself is the *medium* in which to discern subtle energy. Whether a Medical Intuitive reads your body energy for you, or you learn to tune into your own intuition to hear your Self, the subtle senses are a *means* to communicate, what is beyond the conscious minds current knowledge. Medical Intuition in itself is not a healing modality. Medical Intuition as a tool of observation of what the body is expressing, can be very valuable in conjunction with other healing modalities and treatments, because it is working from the premise that the individual in all aspects, is the truest representation and authority of its Self, and what it needs to restore health.

To develop ones own intuition, is to reactivate the innate ability within our own bodies to become a self-healing and self-regulating organism. Each person has within them an individual map that tells the story of the disease state as it has manifested in their physical body. To attend to the body on a sensing level can reveal what the conscious mind is unable to identify as its root cause… because it has forgotten. The root cause lies on the level of the subconscious, unconscious to the individual experiencing the symptoms.

The application of our own Intuitive abilities in relation to our health, to me, is the part of medicine that belongs with each of us to implement. Where Medical Intuition is to observe and report what the body is expressing; to engage our own intuitive abilities in awareness, is to enter the process of healing our Self. Intuitive Healers, sometimes referred to as Spiritual Healers, through developing their extra senses, and an ability to be completely present with the energy of another, are able transcend the limits of time and space to become in essence Selfless. It is through this state of selflessness, that they have the ability to become another energetically, in order to heal them. As we all have the ability to develop our extra senses, and become integrated with our spiritual, mental and physical bodies, it only stands to reason that we all have the ability to heal ourselves, and heal others. Every step we take to become closer to Soul, the higher our own body energy vibrates, as there is less negative energy that has collected within us, that serves to separate us, from the higher vibration of the Soul. The physical body becomes lighter, and becomes a better receptor for higher frequencies, to pass through it. There is less 'muck' in the way, that slows down the vibration of the Soul, as it attempts to extend itself outward from within us. To be focused in the moment, on whatever we are doing, brings that vibration into that moment. The healing is not necessarily an intention to heal another. It is based on the intent to be present with another, authentically attending to what they share with us as it is, not what we think it should be. So whether we work in a corner store, or weed gardens for a living, we all have the potential to heal one another, through being present, and attending to the moment we are living. In our presence, our energy with another becomes harmonious, and the lower frequencies within each are automatically raised to the higher frequencies present. Everyone in this world has the potential inherent to be a healer, whether they define it as such, or not.

To develop ones own intuitive abilities, is to become empowered to heal oneself, with conscious awareness. The residual effect is that all those around us benefit. It is the one part of our healing that we can be responsible for ourselves. To intuitively engage, is to bring consciousness to all that supports the state of health we have chosen on the conscious level. Intuition, through its very nature, has the ability to reveal all that we are operating from without knowledge, or recognition, that is creating our disease state. To work with our subconscious perceptions, intuitively, is to enter in consciousness our state of being, where we become aware of the choices we are making that support health in every moment.

To bring awareness to these unrecognized parts of Self that are not balanced, is to dismantle the nonphysical internal walls that we have created to protect ourselves from a perceived external threat. Physical toxicity can become walled off physically within our bodies, when left unrecognized on the energetic form, where they originated in our thoughts and perceptions. Energetic collections, particularly emotions, compromise the body's ability to function and eliminate efficiently. These unrecognized barriers on the energetic level also serve to compromise the acceptance and positive response to treatment and healing on the physical level. Our inner potential to heal, and the body's ability to regain its natural state of health, can be accessed through intuition, by bringing into awareness all that the body is operating from, subconsciously. In this one act of liberating our unrecognized resistance into awareness, we are once again aligned with our unlimited potential, to meet challenges on the physical, mental and emotional levels again.

This internal wall that represents our resistance on the mental and emotional levels serves to keep us isolated from healing our physical disease. For treatments and therapies to be effective, they have to penetrate the walls we have put up to protect us from perceived threats, both on the physical and energetic levels. In order to reach beyond these perceived limitations, to access the power to heal within, our illusion of isolation must be brought into our conscious awareness. The walls that our physical body has created, in the form or scar tissue and compromised cell permeability, are no longer the body's focus, because the physical body is no longer in the mode of producing a compensation to protect itself. The pathogens are no longer threats as the integrity is reestablished in the physical body. The unknown, which is what the disease represented to the body, is what it is, and nothing more, because it has *not* been predetermined as life threatening. The immune system is now working with the body and recognizing what it needs to address. What we know, we can change, because we are consciously aligned with making a choice that supports health.

Remember the God I spoke of before; the one that is like the nicest guy in the world? He has his hand outstretched, in hopes of us taking his hand, to be pulled through our illusion of separation. Where we feel pain, physically or emotionally, there exists a perception of separation. Maybe this is where many of us getting fooled. Where is God or Goddess exactly? Is God an external or internal experience? If God is perceived as external, then accepting our own resistance to our acceptance of God brings us back to our internal experience. Ultimately, God is both internal and external. To see the Divine at work in our lives, we must first come to experience the Divine at work within us. So, asking ourselves where we perceive God to be, can help us understand where our focus needs to be brought, in order to be pulled through the illusion of separation. To engage intuitively, whether ourselves, or by someone who can read that energy for us, is to reveal the part of Self, that believes it is separate. A decision, or idea we have about that one part of Self, has become encapsulated within us, and we don't even recognize that it is acting through us all the time, in hopes of being recognized on the conscious level. To acknowledge the idea that keeps us separate from accepting the Divine essence within our own being, is to bring integrity back to Soul, where we may become empowered to meet our challenges. If God is within, than to heal we must trust, that when we allow ourselves to accept and feel discomfort inside ourselves, we become closer to the center of our being. This one step alone brings us to what we least expect, because every part of us is related. In that instant of recognition, we become the center of each cell, the center of a tumor, the center of a thought, the center of our current experience, and there, God/Goddess will be to receive us. We know we have found the Divine within, because in that moment, we are enveloped in the incredible experience of Love. The truth of the Divine in reality is not internal, or external, as it is Oneness with our own Essence, our Soul. It is merely the perception, of being one way or the other, in its limitation that serves to keep us separate, from knowing this core truth through experience.

Meeting our resistance is like being at the gates to heaven. By acknowledging our pain, and feelings of separation in honesty, is to be received into the garden of God. In accepting what we honestly feel at a deep level, even though we don't want to feel that way, or recognize that we could hold such feelings, is to surrender to guidance. Our false perceptions, judgments and current resistance must be left with humility outside such a sacred healing space. Only truth survives within God's sanctuary, for it is all that can set us free emotionally, mentally and physically from our state of discomfort and be led to a greater experience of ourselves. Where there is Love, there is acceptance and understanding. The illusions that have been created by our own fears dissolve. Pure and simple honesty takes us there. It is in our ease, we accept and resonate with all that heals. God's hand is always there for us, as he never closes any gates. We don't only perceive closed gates, but we actually create the gates with our perceptions of separation. Heaven is not separate, nor is the sacred reserved for a garden with gates that one has limited access to. The peace of heaven remains separate and invisible as long as we perceive threat, fear, doubt and pain that can't be accepted, and in turn relinquished, to see what is beyond it, in its truth. If we think of our pain and fear as signposts that the gate is there for us, whether we believe God is within us, or outside our being, doesn't matter. Either way, we have to face the inevitable. We have to summon the courage to step right into the middle of our pain, and fear, in order to be received into the inner sanctuary of Oneness with God. Once we have the courage to enter the unknown, and step right into the pain and face the fear, there is nothing there, as it is an illusion. It is only through the act of embracing and accepting the pain and fear as our current reality, that the illusion is revealed to us, and all that remains is truth. As the illusion is revealed, in its truth, we see there is no gate, there is no pain, there remains only gratitude, for we are immersed in peace, and the experience of Love. The illusion of false perceptions, blind one to the truth that God is everywhere! Without gates and walls of resistance, there is only peace, and disease does not exist anymore, as we are no longer separate from the highest truth of our being. We are all God in its many expressions… each of us full of goodness and grace in our uniqueness.

The physical symptom of our true state of disease, is what we call the Cancer, the Multiple Sclerosis, the Rheumatoid Arthritis, and all the named Diagnosis, as we have come to define them. These are the physical representations that our body has come to express for us to recognize that there is something terribly wrong going on within us. The physical manifestation for most needs biochemical intervention of some form in order to change it, but the true source has started on the energetic level of our being, and needs to be related to in a form it recognizes and accepts, in order to truly resolve. To treat the physical, without the energetic, is to be limited in addressing the true state of disease. The concept of utilizing the power of presence, to bring about transformation, is what Energy Medicine is aligned with. The theory of applying force to resolve an existing symptom, such as Chemotherapy or Radiation, has historically been the approach of Allopathic Medicine. Why do we have to have one or the other? If *disease* is the issue here, than is it possible both of these represent the polarities of the same state? …the state of separation, from our comfort and peace within. To actualize the potential of healing, would it not make sense that the individual in their unique expression of their state of disease, and their unique collection of perceptions and beliefs, would require different combinations of physical, and energetic approaches, to find balance, in order to regain a state of health? Depending on their ability to be present with themselves, at the depth of perception that would facilitate transforming their state of disease, the ratio of one approach, versus the other, may be different. If one has a limited ability to perceive Self, then intervention through biochemical approaches will be necessary, to reinitiate their body's ability to overcome the threat that disease poses, for the survival of the physical body. The symptom of disease may respond well to this intervention, but unless it is continued, it will be a matter of time before the causal level that is left unresolved on the energetic level, will manifest itself again in another recognizable symptom.

The catch is this: for many advanced pathologies, our receptor for these senses has been shut down, or is not operating properly. The Pineal gland is the physical receptor we each have that connects us with our intuition. With Cancer, and autoimmune processes, this gland has become compromised and isn't reliably relaying information to our physical body. In the current state of imbalance, in the functioning of the Pineal Gland, we don't trust the feelings we do have, as there is no clarity. The ability to discern Self from others is compromised, as the physical body is operating, in isolation. To make decisions, about which therapies, and what interventions we choose to facilitate our healing of the physical body, is very difficult if we have no reference, for what is ultimately in our heart, to invest in. The Pineal Gland is the 'gland of emotion', and it connects us with our inner feelings, and our Sensitivity, on the level of extra sensory awareness. With serious pathologies, the Pineal Gland is not operating. We are energetically cut off from our feelings altogether. The gate to heaven appears to be a heavily bricked wall with guards standing outside, with firearms pointed directly at us. The physical body is operating in a state of overwhelm, and subtle energy in the form of emotional wisdom, is not even part of the equation. Survival is the only focus. Without the Pineal Gland operating efficiently, it is difficult to feel anything, let alone subtle energy, or the truth within ourselves about how we feel, about anything we experience. We sometimes need support to learn to hear our hearts again, so we can make sense of where we are, in relation to where we want to be, in our state of optimum health.

I have had patients come into my office asking me what they should do. They have been diagnosed with Cancer, or an autoimmune disease, and up until that time they had no experience, or understanding of what it meant to be seriously ill. They have been given a prognosis that does not give hope to regaining a healthy state again. All that they do know is that they want to live, and be healthy again, and it doesn't seem possible with the choices they are given. On a conscious level, they are operating from the belief that they want to live in health again, but their body is operating from a completely different program. They are unknowingly being influenced by the body's hidden program, set up for self-destruction because they can't feel within, how their body is responding to their choices. None of us would consciously choose to have such a program running on its own if we were in knowledge of it.

Somewhere along the line we separate from a part of our Self, without realizing it, because it makes us uncomfortable to be with it. This part we cannot resolve, is left as a pocket of energy inside us, safely stashed away to keep us functioning on the conscious level efficiently, or so we tell ourselves. We leave that pocket of energy to combat all the physical threats that our bodies deal with on a daily basis in isolation, cut off from the integrity of the body systems that are operating with resources. To live in our toxic environment, cell phones, electromagnetic fields, pesticides, chemicals, pollutants, chemical additives and preservatives in our food and manufactured goods, we need to be efficient, at keeping what has the potential to harm us physically, from becoming contained in us. These pockets of energy are in their essence representative of our dis*ease* state, and with the introduction of the physical toxicity from our environment, and consumption through food, and everyday household products; the body becomes contaminated and overloaded. Over time, we manifest symptoms such as Cancer and autoimmune disorders that are the body's attempt to preserve its integrity.

There are specialists in the natural and conventional fields of medicine for each of these diseases that have skills that can be utilized to help resolve these symptoms. However, the actual healing and resolution must ultimately be faced on the energy level, in order to completely transform them into something that supports, and empowers us, in our state of health. To benefit from the expertise of the specific methods of treatment and therapies, whether they are natural or conventional, there is still the aspect of healing that we are left with day-to-day to overcome ourselves. And from a preventative position, through awareness, we can address the source of toxicity, and disease present in our environment, and ourselves, that as a society we have the power to change. To address the root cause of these symptoms requires becoming aware and proactive with our choices, both on an energetic level, and on a material level. Environmental awareness is a reflection of the awareness of the individuals who are part of our Society. There are therapists who can help us with our part of the healing process, but ultimately it is our responsibility to face what is within us that is unresolved, so we can come to be aware, of what is external that supports our health. As people become physically less overwhelmed by toxicity and congestion, they naturally move towards entering the subtle levels of discomfort, within their perceptions. Facilitating my patients to regain health has brought on its coattails, the natural development of my model for the Process of Inner Alchemy.

We have become so specialized in our professions that for the new comer to illness it is overwhelming to try and decipher which approaches and philosophies are going to work for them. Most in the state of overwhelm, are not able to know, or sense, or feel, what is best for them to do, and are in a state of pain, confusion and vulnerability. The Process of Inner Alchemy is to help bring structure, and understanding to the part of our health, we can take responsibility for, our innate ability to be Self-regulating, Self-healing organisms, when aligned with our potential. The process of transforming disease, into peace and comfort within, is the part that we each have the ability to participate in, so we can benefit from all the areas of expertise, including professionals, with skills and knowledge beyond our own that can help to bring us to the state of health again.

In simple terms, if we understand that we are not powerless in the face of illness, nor are we powerless in our current experience of life, we align with the potential within, rather then remaining victims of circumstance. We all have within us the innate ability to heal if actualized, and at the least, if not fully actualized, we have the ability to discern, what best facilitates us on our personal pathway back to health, and experience of joy in our lives. Intuition is our internal guide that allows us to unveil truth for ourselves. When we find our truth, it all seems to make perfect sense to us. With these extra senses engaged, we can better discern, that which has the ability to threaten our survival, on the physical level. Our trusted instincts about toxicity, and dangerous environments, reveal to us our part in supporting them. With intuition engaged, we are aligned with the knowledge that has the ability to change them, rather than becoming victim to them.

Hopefully, in sharing where my understanding has taken me, you will connect with all that serves your highest good, and the truth within you, that sets you free to be in your power, with your intuitive abilities right there at your side to guide you. Intuition connects you with your Soul again, and there are infinite possibilities, when you can come to know and experience, your own truth in its clarity. Intuition is a means to find the answers within yourself that empower you in any challenging life experience.

THE BIG PICTURE

Humanity is mourning right now. To remember our truth is more important then ever because the greater the discord, and upheaval, the greater the potential for transformation. To do this, we must expose our misconceptions, so that we may embrace a greater reality for ourselves, one where we may celebrate one another, and experience the Wholeness of being in touch with our true Essence. Health is an integral part of this Earth experience. This mourning is perhaps in response to realizing we have forsaken the greatest truth we all carry within us. The truth is, that we are free to experience our Essence in the human form, and to experience one another in our magnificence with all of our gifts. Our gifts together, working in harmony, have the ability to heal what we have harmed here on Earth. In taking responsibility for our part in it, we may all be elevated to a greater consciousness, where the pain and isolation that exists, no longer serves to move us to realize what we are doing to ourselves. We will be inspired to a greater experience, through awareness of our actions, and participation in its creation. Collectively, this is our world, and we can experience it anyway we choose. This is the power of the individual's mind to create filters for what we choose to see and participate in. The more we learn to focus our thoughts and understand the dimensions of our mind, the more we will be consciously part of life as it really exists, and understand our contribution to it. It becomes difficult to act in harmful and destructive ways towards our environment, and one another, when we are consciously aware of our part in the Whole, and come to observe the effects of our actions taken disconnected from awareness.

Developing intuition is to venture outside the cage of our current conscious mind, into the realm of the unknown, to rediscover the vastness and experience of possibility, and truth, which is our birthright. It is through this doorway, that we can come to trust our minds again, and in turn our Soul again, so we can access the means to heal ourselves, in body, mind and Spirit. Aligned with Soul, we are empowered to hear our individual roadmap back to health, for Soul is never diminished in its perfection. Our Soul knows exactly what we need, in order to heal the Self. All we have to do is remember the language in which the Soul expresses itself, and summon the courage to live and speak our truth, as it is revealed to us through the aspects of Self we have come to believe represent who we are. We have adopted a false sense of Self, through collective consciousness, which when not realized in its truth, serves to create our state of disease by separating us from the greater truth of our Soul.

PART THREE:
The Process of Inner Alchemy

The Process of Inner Alchemy is about the journey within to transform what no longer serves us in its current expression, into a fuller and more integrated expression of who we really are in awareness, aligned with our Soul's potential. The Process of Inner Alchemy is about the path of transformation that leads us to the experience of Wholeness and Oneness with All. On this path we embrace the parts of ourselves that need to be healed in order to experience a greater reality for ourselves. I believe it is not the current experience that is our greatest threat, but the subconscious beliefs that are imprinted in our cells that trigger us in the present without our awareness of where they are coming from that is the real threat. Our physical bodies develop symptoms as a way to express what yearns to be healed on a deeper level of our being. Over time we develop compensations in our everyday life that we don't recognize. If we move beyond our comfort zone into what we currently perceive to be our limitations, be it pain, fear, or actual obstacles that are before us, and replace these with possibilities, what would that mean? We would be free to experience a greater reality of ourselves in a Conscious State of Awareness.

In defining the levels in which we are able to perceive, and the components of our awareness, we are able to bring reference to our experience as we consciously embark on the journey of unveiling our truth to come into the experience of our Soul. When we embark on the journey within, it is the emotions that become our greatest allies, and also our greatest deceivers. They have the ability to keep us engaged in the illusions we have created or adopted unconsciously by giving us a false sense of our current reality. By acknowledging our emotions as a valid expression of something that lies hidden beneath, they have the ability to act as beacons that can lead us back to the natural state of peace and joy.

We come to trust these beacons as valid guidance towards something within that we need to reclaim in order to feel complete. So begins the transformation from limitations to infinite possibilities. Without limitations what initially remains, is a world we have little reference for or acknowledgement for, from the exterior. Our validation becomes reliant completely on an internal experience. As we come to trust this inner guidance, intuition, we also come to see our external world as merely a reflection of our internal state.

What if we were free to be who we are in our potential? Is it possible that in our potential we would also come to recognize others in their potential? Inner Alchemy is the journey within, and as we work through the Levels of Awareness we come to find our Essence, the level of the Soul. It is here, at the Essence, that we find one another in OUR Essence as well. We are led back to the Source of All, but to connect with it we must go inward. When we reach it, the external and internal becomes ONE and our sense of Self becomes Selfless. I believe we have a truer knowledge of our True Selves, and our Soul, connected to Source than any other level of physical existence. What limitations would remain to keep us from healing on all levels? I believe none.

Inner Alchemy requires us to be in our truth, wherever that may currently be, while summoning the courage to relinquish any ownership over it, to open the doors to the possibility that there is more to perceive in awareness. Our mind has the ability to reveal exactly what needs healing in the body, where it originates and what it represents in our current perception of reality. Learning to trust our mind and its abilities is a huge leap of faith for most of us, but once taken, perceptions emerge that we can't believe we lived without experiencing consciously before. The leap of faith is the biggest hurdle, because the rest is just like baby steps. We all came into this world to learn the basic functions of our human form. Now, we have the opportunity to take what we are able to know of our body sensations and integrate what we knew at birth about our extra sensory abilities. There is nothing to learn

The Process of Inner Achemy

here, it is a step-by-step process of remembering what has been functioning in isolation from our conscious mind. I have given the levels to perception as a guide to take you from one level that you consciously know, to the next level, through tuning into what the body is revealing through its subtle energy. It is easy, so easy in fact you will feel you are making it up as you go. It is not until you reach the point of revelation that your physical body shifts and there is a sensation of lightness and freedom that takes over your awareness. There is no denying its validity once you have experienced the power of the Soul as you reconnect with its magnificence. This therapy can be done many times to transform all that no longer serves you in your health and wellbeing. For every step we take forward in our experience of life, our vibration increases, and all that is below that vibration no longer can lay dormant in the subconscious without creating recognizable resistance. It is this resistance we become aware of without realizing its origin as within us.

Through the Process of Inner Alchemy we come to have conscious awareness about our Self in its many aspects, and ultimately with these aspects working in harmony, we come to connect with Soul consciously where we experience what it is to be Selfless. We come to realize what beliefs and conditioned modes of functioning we are operating from, not just on a physical level, but mental and emotional levels as well that no longer serve us in moving forward in our life. Through Inner Alchemy we have the opportunity to go in to retrieve the parts of our Self that we have missed developing, experiencing and rejoicing in along the way. We aren't rewriting experience, or changing it in its truth, we are acknowledging the part it played in providing enough discomfort to fuel growth and development of an aspect of us that otherwise would have lay dormant. In this realization of a greater truth, we are able to embrace the gift that it carried on its wings. Our wounds, our trauma, our injustices, are like the angels within, in disguise; carrying on their wings our yet to be realized Essence in it's freeform.

DEFINING OUR CURRENT PERCEPTIONS

Our current perceptions are how we see ourselves, and how we experience ourselves in various situations. Our current perceptions are what we have come to believe we are on the conscious level. When information is presented to us, we automatically receive it in certain ways, without even realizing the level at which we are assimilating, and experiencing it. When I first began working with patients intuitively, I wondered how some people were able to easily receive from me information about what their body was expressing, and others had a difficult time relating to the information that was coming from their body, through a Medical Intuitive Scan. When I do a Medical Intuitive Scan, the information presents itself in different ways, depending on the individual, and the way their body expresses it's Self. I intuitively knew, that if the information came from within them, they would automatically resonate with how their body was expressing their information, and consciously begin to develop a relationship with it, having received it on the cognitive level. In hindsight, I feel a little foolish for not understanding that the bridge between where we are consciously operating from, and the subconscious programming that runs our body, is not always anchored on either end, to anything that makes sense to us, or we have taken time to acknowledge. Let's face it; we live in a time where the intellect is on overdrive. To hear how we feel, and what we are experiencing on a deeper level, meets deaf ears for anyone functioning on the "need to know what to do about it," information highway. We are so focused on taking action that we have forgotten where the directives for our actions come from. We are invested in outcomes, instead of focusing on the moment, and what we bring to it of ourselves. Are we short-changing our experience of full potential by predetermining what we expect to achieve?

If we invest in bringing our best to whatever we do, would we not recognize our discomfort in the form it initially expresses itself? Initially, either through the intellects perceptions, the emotions, or the

The Process of Inner Achemy

body sensations we become aware of not being comfortable. Depending on which of these we are aware of, we can begin to appreciate, that we are limited in experiencing our current experience in its entirety. How many of us ignore these uncomfortable perceptions, and push on towards our goal believing it is the situation, or another person that is making it difficult for us? If we do become aware of our discomfort, in its subtler forms of expression, we are better equipped to seek answers within, then ignoring it, and spending our energy on creating compensations to function efficiently, despite our discomfort. The body will automatically compensate, and develop symptoms that reflect its imbalance, in hopes of being recognized in its discomfort. Often, not until it reaches a physical symptom do we have awareness about our discomfort, as something internally that is real to us. In our state of disease, it is our inability to relate to the discomfort within ourselves on the subtler energetic levels in the first place that has created the manifestation of our current diagnosed disease, or uncomfortable symptoms. For those with serious pathology, the perception is not of being *in* the state of disease rather of *having* a disease, which suggests it is separate from us, because we haven't developed a way to personally have relationship to it. We have unconsciously operated from the state of disease, without any knowledge of it's influence, or ability to recognize it as something that doesn't belong with our True Self. It is very difficult for any of us to see what is simply right before us when we are in the midst of it. I came to find that missing piece needed to help my patients relate to the intuitive information their body was expressing to me. It is one thing, if we intuitively connect with our own bodies, as there is cohesiveness naturally formed, as the intuitive skills are developed. But to receive the information from an outside source, can often be misinterpreted if there is no way to relate to it, as it is being expressed. Part of them may resonate with it, but often, it triggers the very resistance that has kept it neatly compartmentalized within them to begin with. It can feel rather exposing, to have someone tell you, what you believed was private and unknowable by anyone else. I attended a lecture of Dr. Rajan Sankaran, a Homeopathic Doctor from India, and author of several books on Homeopathy.

The first day of Dr. Sankaran's lecture he presented an outline of his work he has defined by the "Levels of Experience." I immediately resonated with the list of levels he presented as his foundation for prescribing homeopathic remedies. In my own process, I had not recognized the importance of defining the levels that we perceive, in bridging the gap between our current conscious perceptions, and our potential for expanded conscious awareness. In hearing his presentation, it occurred to me that to define the intuitive process for the intellect would create a sense of safety to embrace in awareness, what was currently thought to be unchartered territory. It became clear to me that with resistance on the mental level removed, integration of the two ends of the spectrum, current conscious perceptions and expanded conscious awareness, is not only possible but also attainable with ease. Working intuitively with people had left me wondering how to better facilitate another to build relationship with what their body was expressing on a subconscious level. To heal, one needs awareness of themselves, and their needs, in order to facilitate their body to respond to treatment. In the midst of it, I had missed the obvious. To build relationship to how people currently process information would minimize resistance, as they are guided toward an expanded awareness.

Dr. Sankaran's presentation of the defined "Levels of Experience" inspired me to study further the work of the late New York Psychologist, Dr. Abraham Maslow who developed the original five level "Hierarchy of Human Needs" Model between 1943 and 1954. Dr. Maslow said the following, *"Self Actualization is the intrinsic growth of what is already in the organism, or more accurately, of what the organism is."* It is interesting to note that Dr. Maslow's research and study was done exclusively on healthy people, rather than unhealthy ones.

To go back a step further it was Dr. Kurt Goldstein, a German Neurologist, who had originated the idea of Self-actualization in his famous book, *The Organism*, (1934).

"We have said that life confronts us in living organisms. But as soon as we attempt to grasp them scientifically, we must take them apart, and this taking apart nets us a multitude of isolated facts, which offer no direct clue to that which we experience directly in the living organism. Yet we have no way of making the nature and behavior of an organism scientifically intelligible other than by its construction out of facts obtained in this way. We thus face the basic problem of all biology, possibly of all knowledge. The question can be formulated quite simply: What do the phenomena, arising from the isolating procedure, teach us about the "Essence" (the intrinsic nature) of an organism? How, from such phenomena, do we come to an understanding of the behavior of the individual organism?" Kurt Goldstein, *The Organism*, p. 7 (1963 edition)

Returning to some of the models I had previously studied revealed a synchronicity between what intuitively I had been working with, and creating a specific framework, that would facilitate sharing my work with the Process of Inner Alchemy for others to be able to do for themselves. Just as I do a Medical Intuitive Scan of another, the Process of Inner Alchemy is also based on following the energy, through the levels of perception, to reach the Essence of the disease state in awareness. There is nothing new in this basic concept, as my research revealed, but our ability to apply the knowledge of these pioneers has evolved significantly as human consciousness has increased.

I've developed the following diagram as a visual to accompany this chapter. If we begin with the levels of perception, and initiate exploration into the realm of the unknown, it is helpful to expand our understanding of our currently held perceptions, to include our broadening awareness. This diagram is symbolic of the ripples of consciousness. Each ripple in its evolution of awareness has a direct relationship with the currently held perception. From the center, in conscious awareness of our Essence, or Soul, we are directly in touch with The Source of All. The intensity of Soul, is like the innate seed of potential that is our part of the Source of All. Through the layers of perception, or life conditioning, this Essence becomes diluted until it is reduced to being a Name and Description that represents Collective Consciousness. It still carries the same true Essence, but it is no longer *pure Essence,* as it has been disguised in the illusion of what collectively, as a human race, we have come to interpret it as, through our intellect. We have become such experts intellectually, that we have completely forgotten our common sense, the language of the Soul. From one end of the spectrum, to the other, in our perceptions, we are given the opportunity, to once again bring Wholeness, to our experience of who we are, by engaging in awareness of subtle energy. In following the energy of the body, we are led by the subtle senses, to bring expanded awareness to the current perceptions that create distance between who we believe we are through conditioning, and the truth of our Soul.

The Process of Inner Achemy

THE RELATIONSHIP BETWEEN CURRENT PERCEPTIONS & EXTRA SENSORY AWARENESS

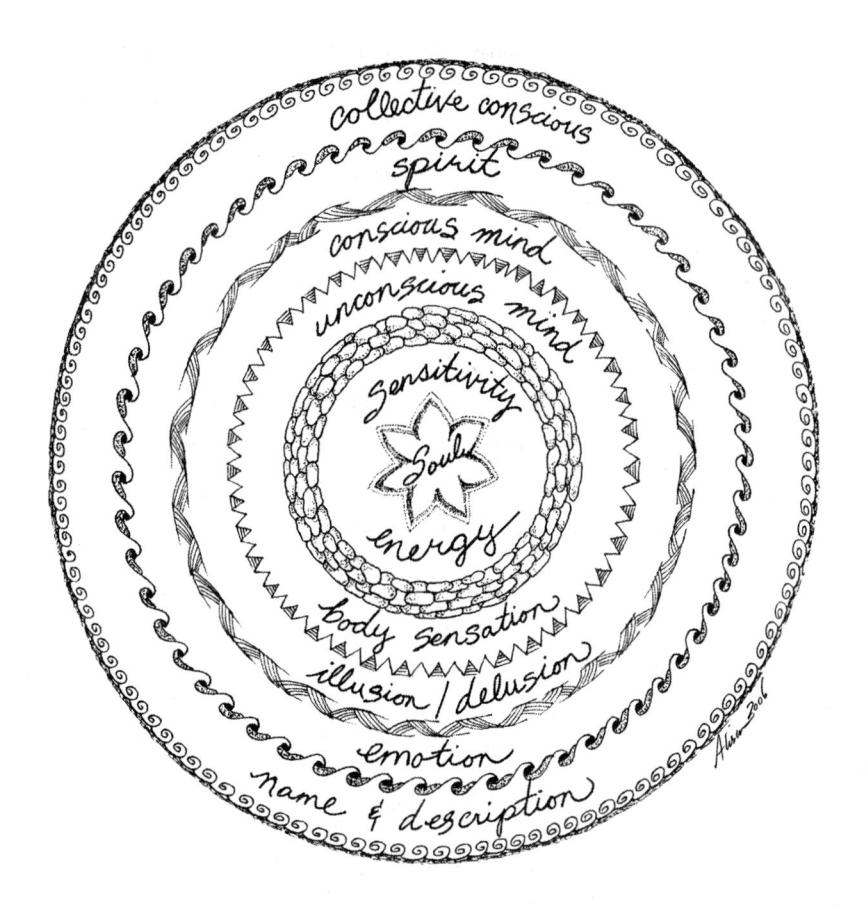

(concentric circles, from outermost to innermost:)
- collective conscious
- spirit
- conscious mind
- unconscious mind
- sensitivity
- Soul
- energy
- body sensation
- illusion / delusion
- emotion
- name & description

THE LEVELS OF PERCEPTION

How many of us go along, without really allowing time to ponder, just how we look at things, and how the outcomes we experience, have a direct relationship to these perceptions. If you are afraid of failing a test, are you're efforts generated from believing you will succeed, or are you completely caught up with all the reasons its not possible for you to be successful. When you do fail, are you surprised? In not acknowledging what you invested your time, energy and thoughts into in preparation for the test, does it not further endorse your original belief? We all do this everyday, without even recognizing it. And those of us who do realize it, how do we stop automatically buying into such outcomes for ourselves? We can consciously change our actions, but it takes sheer will power to change our natural way of operating. There is an easier way, but first we have to recognize what we do know of ourselves, and catch what impressions come flying through our minds, when we are confronted with challenge. There are levels to how we recognize these impressions. Our health directly reflects how we have come to unknowingly perceive ourselves, in the same way. How many people are afraid of getting cancer? They think of it like it's something you catch. The only thing you are going to get, through harboring this unrecognized fear, is the mentality that predisposes us to cancer. In not recognizing our fear, we continue consuming toxic products without thinking about it, and unknowingly expose ourselves to harmful environments and habits. Our bodies respond by creating what we do recognize as threatening, cancer. We all perceive our reality, and ourselves individually, and develop health states that can help us to define where we have created separation from our Wholeness. For many at this time, this separation is being accentuated by very devastating Diseases. Not only are these Diseases a reflection of our separation from our true potential as humans, but also our diseases reflect the environment we have created that is toxic and detrimental to maintaining a state of physical health. In the journey of Self-actualization, there are steps that represent the level at which we perceive our Self, and others, that are common to all of us on the journey. In defining these levels of perception, it becomes easier to recognize the limitations we place in our way to finding a greater experience of health for ourselves.

Perhaps the most helpful thing about defining these levels of perceptions is the acknowledgement that we are commonly seeking something that is beyond our ability to think through, rationalize and justify to others. There are no words that can amply explain or define what we find at the level of the highest truth. It is an experience and every person has the ability to achieve it, but we have our conscious mind along with us and it requires some sense of safety, some sense of reason to be able to change its mind about how we see things. Health is our natural state. Healing is always possible when we place our focus on achieving it. I am going to place this exploration in the context of health, because that is the area that my life work has taken me. Of course you can apply this to fulfillment, career, family, anything that we experience involves this same process. With each level of perception, we come one step closer to realizing our potential as multi-sensory beings, with the ability to embrace our gifts and contribute consciously to the whole of humanity.

THE NAME

Our physical health seems to be taken for granted as long as we are able to function and do the things we want in comfort. Today we have so many people with Autoimmune Disorders, Cancer, High Blood Pressure, Hormonal Imbalances and a myriad of diagnosed health conditions. These are names we have given to health states that present a certain picture through their symptoms. To name them is to give them a commonly agreed on diagnosis, but it is limited to what society as a whole, and the medical community have agreed they represent. There are perceived outcomes, and ways in which the disease state can be treated, under this method of diagnosis. The common belief is that through intervention they can be treated, contained and hopefully eradicated from our bodies. Through this belief the responsibility for their treatment comes to rest on the shoulders of the medical community. There are times this approach works very well and because of the faith placed in the Doctors and Caregivers the disease is resolved or at least effectively treated to control its further development.

Naming the disease state for many is very comforting because it puts into context something that is beyond our ability to comprehend and safely takes the responsibility and places it with someone we feel knows more than us. It serves to keep us in the place of being the recipient of illness. It has happened to us, not created by us, and therefore we are at the mercy of others to fix it for us. There is an initial relief that the feelings of discomfort being experienced are recognizable by someone other than us, and they know just what to do to get rid of them. When we name a health condition we automatically draw on a collective belief about that particular condition. Cancer, for instance, immediately sets off bells of having a disease that is very difficult to control, and that the ultimate expected outcome is death. With so much Cancer among us it is interesting that we can buy into the mentality of believing it is the same for everyone diagnosed with it. The label of a disease summarizes an experience into a known simple recognizable description. We have further broken it down to be Lung Cancer, Prostate Cancer, Ovarian Cancer, Breast Cancer and many more, but in general they ultimately all share a commonly believed prognosis. It is a matter of how effective the treatments are for each, and if the development of the disease can be contained or slowed down. With the label there is no personal relationship developed with the diagnosis. It is as if it belonged to everyone, and our personal part in it is innocent. We hand over any alliance with it to the accepted authorities to deal with, to separate it from us, and therefore saving us from that which is threatening our survival, so we can resume our life as we were before.

THE DESCRIPTION

After being given a diagnosis, there is information that goes hand in hand with its name. There are the ideas that are presented as facts to us about the particular disease. In other words, the facts are the elements that have become commonly experienced by many with the same diagnosis. They further help to describe the name given in terms of where it is, what it looks like, all the information that are the known facts about the particular condition. With both of these levels of perception, the name and the description, there is no personal connection to the disease. They are complete in their common understanding and accepted as what we have and how it is described and identified. Often we search for a diagnosis to gain better understanding of what we are experiencing as defined by others with knowledge of the similar experience. Somehow we find safety in knowing we are not alone with our discomfort, and are given guidelines to express it through others identifying it and describing it for us. It doesn't occur to us to seek understanding beyond what has been presented as factual.

THE EMOTION

To take a step further with our perceptions we enter the emotional component that is how we feel about it. The feelings of sadness, anger, fear, worry and a myriad of emotions that really have nothing to do with the facts or description of an experience. They are our personal response to what is going on with us on a deeper level. To feel our emotions, is to start to break free of what the name and description have defined by a common belief, to be our experience. Our emotions are what begin to make the experience personal to us. This is also the place that we can become "stuck" so easily because emotions can be very powerful and we can feel overwhelmed by them. We begin to experience not being in control of ourselves, or safe in entering our emotions, as they make no sense to the intellect. It seems easier to avoid getting caught up in our emotions by sticking to the facts when making decisions. The emotions lead us into the realm of the intangible where we are unable to express our experience in factual terms. To depersonalize our state of health initially, makes us feel more in control and better able to cope. To acknowledge how we feel is to accept that we are human and have emotions and that we have something inside us we have no understanding of, or reference for, and feels uncontrollable. The acknowledgement of our emotions, whatever they may be, is an important step towards facing our fear that there are circumstances we have no control over. We keep the integrity of the perception of being the victim in tact by denying our emotions.

In entering the level of emotion with our perceptions we begin to connect with ourselves and it is validated with the realization that we are IN the state of disEASE not recipients of it. Embracing the concept of becoming responsible for ourselves, and the choices we make, is now just over the horizon, even though we can't see it yet. The emotional level is like being in the thick of our experience, not knowing which direction will take us out and what we should do because our emotions are not founded in the world of the rational. The emotions can be the muck of life. Everything becomes personal, even when it is not intended to be by others. Emotions can be horrible, or they can be wonderful. Emotions are very difficult to have validated from the external, because they belong to the realm of our personal internal world. They don't always make sense but they are real to us. Only we can acknowledge their validity, by accepting that they represent the first level of how we perceive things, as they are experienced by us, on a personal level.

THE ILLUSION

An Illusion is something that deceives the senses or mind. It is a false belief, idea or concept about something, that makes our perception of something appear to exist, when in fact it does not. It is how we have come to collectively define particular aspects of Self, our experience, and our perceptions of certain circumstances. Illusion is fantasy, and can be a common experience, romanticized. It is how we see ourselves and what we identify with. The archetypes, or aspects of Self, are active within us at this level of perception. For example, we can see ourselves as the victim, the rescuer, the healer, the wounded child, the mother, the wife, or a myriad of other identities, within a given situation. When we identify with these aspects of Self we see only what supports that illusion, and miss the actual truth of ourselves, in the situation. The illusion is our unconsciously adopted reality.

An Illusion, by justifying its existence, has the ability to keep an aspect of our Self from becoming actualized into a fuller expression of our being. The illusion is that we are defined by these known expressions, that collectively we have come to recognize, as experience. We share these perceptions without conscious awareness of their influence over how we experience ourselves. The aspects of Self each carry certain collective beliefs and perceptions of who we are in a particular circumstance and we actually believe they are who we are. We have our personal renditions of common illusions, or delusions, based on how we personally see our reality from our experience in it, but illusions are common to many, and endorsed by mankind. Simply put, an illusion, or our delusion, is a false sense of reality. An illusion is a limited perception because it is only one part of an aspect of Self acknowledged, within any given circumstance. It is not Self, connected to Wholeness. It is just the part we choose to see to keep ourselves feeling understood and recognized in an acceptable way. It can serve to unconsciously justify continuing in the same direction we are headed, because it is recognized and understood by many. It serves to keep us momentarily feeling comfortable, and feeling that we are Whole, but this is why it is an illusion. Without external enforcement, and acknowledgement, it creates the feeling of void, when we are alone.

An example of an illusion is our shared perceptions of what it is to be a good mother. A woman with a career who isn't home on time to make dinner, or misses her children's music recital because she has something at the office keep her, wrestles with herself because of an ingrained belief that she has not fulfilled her role as a good mother. This may be true, but in operating automatically with these common misperceptions being subconscious, we have already made an assessment, based on what our expectations are of the woman in those situations. For a woman who is a mother that is true to herself, remains clear with her authentic Self, in order to actualize herself within the role of mother, regardless of how it may appear to others. She will surely fall short of meeting the criteria set by others, unaware of her individual circumstance, or her unique abilities. Maybe she can't cook every night, but is very creative in problem solving. In acting from awareness of what is important to us, consciously chosen, and bringing awareness to what may be influencing us subconsciously, we are able to break free of the conflict that the two may evoke, when we step outside the accepted criteria for our roles.

What is a good mother? One who follows the checklist of what is expected of her, or one that brings herself in her many expressions forward into the role of mother? She may bring great value in what she does share with her children, beyond being the audience for their achievements. In following her heart, she may in fact be helping them realize their own achievements, by her demonstration of her own strengths, and contribution to them, in unconventional ways.

Another illusion that is subtle in its influence, is assuming that when someone gives us a gesture of kindness, they must have a hidden agenda. When someone comes forward unexpectedly, and offers to help us, we may feel obliged to reciprocate, instead of graciously accepting their gift, as it was intended, a gesture of kindness or gratitude for us. Or a complete stranger offering to help in an unusual situation raises suspicion; because we think of all the ways they could hurt us, or take advantage of us. We have become conditioned by stories, or knowledge of another's unpleasant experience, without seeing the situation for what it is, for us personally, in that situation. Any one of these things could be true, but do we know that ahead of time? Our preconditioned response is based on illusion that we don't recognize as an influence, in that moment.

The criteria, for successfully fulfilling our roles, and identities of Self, has become defined over time by our ancestors, as are our assumptions about certain situations. Those same identities and roles have become adapted over time, by those that dared step beyond what had been previously defined, by the expectations of society. Collectively our consciousness has evolved by those that went beyond what was previously endorsed as recognizable and acceptable. It is very difficult to experience the true light in another if we have already determined what they represent to us. An illusion is the way we choose to perceive our experience in a particular situation, and it is a shared perception common to all of humanity. The shared perception does not mean that we are not able to be free of it, but as long as we operate with unconscious perceptions influencing us, we can experience conflict within our current situation, when we make choices to grow on a conscious level.

Illusion is not all bad! The use of illusion can help to liberate us from difficult situations as well. Such as when we watch a great movie and we identify with the hero, it can create inspiration and courage to engage that aspect within ourselves that can overcome challenge, and in turn engage that belief to meet our current life hurdle. The illusion that the positive aspect of that character portrays can be helpful for us if it aligns us with a strength within ourselves that otherwise lay dormant, and acts as a catalyst to experience our situation in another way.

The illusion, in this case, is a greater experience of Self than previously existed, but it is still limited to the aspect of Self, rather than aligned with our own Wholeness. For in Wholeness, this same illusion creates boundaries for our own full experience of Self, aligned with Soul. At the level of Soul, the particular aspect of Self, actualized, is no longer engaged; therefore the identity is moved from a "sense of Self" to Selflessness. We become free to be *real* in the moment, as it actually exists.

In the state of delusion, we are operating in a role without recognizing the unconsciously adopted criteria we are attempting to satisfy. The delusion, ultimately serves to hinder our development, by keeping us aligned with something that suppresses, and makes us feel inadequate, in the face of our challenges, because we have not brought our True Self into awareness. We are comparing ourselves to what we subconsciously believe is the ideal expression of that aspect of Self, be it mother, caregiver, teacher or provider. In acknowledging each level of perception, comes the opportunity to discover a deeper connection, with who we really are. When we can accept the way we *feel* on the emotional level in a situation, we are brought to the level of the illusion being revealed. It is right there to be perceived, without the confusion of emotion, pulling at us to conform to what others expect of us in the situation, in order to remain comfortable. Our emotions, when not accepted, act as a fog that conceals our full reality from us, and separates us from seeing things the way they really are. An illusion is a perception that can be of positive or negative influence, depending on how we consciously perceive it, and integrate it into our experience. Illusion as a perception has polarities, whereas illusion in conscious awareness is realized as part of the full spectrum of experience. The polarities, or the dualism of Self has been reconciled, and the veil of illusion is removed, so we see things in their truth, not through the filters of limited Self, as endorsed externally.

This one shift in our perceptions can reactivate our bodies to address the imbalances that sustain the state of disease, and the symptom, so that treatment can become an act of power rather than a fight against something that is within us. Often we are carriers of an illusion subconsciously, without even recognizing it at all, let alone as beneficial or detrimental, until we come to experience the effects of it. If energy manifests into the physical, would it not make sense that how we express and deal with our perceptions would have a direct relationship to how our body functions and regulates itself? As energetic beings, it doesn't make sense that each person is an isolated body that functions completely separately from everyone else. We all share what we can't see, as well as what we do see in manifest form around us. This realization implies that common diseases are in truth, common perceptions, that we have collectively adopted and allowed to manifest through lack of awareness, of what sustains them in our own reality. In other words, what we focus on consciously, and do unconsciously, can align us unknowingly, with the very things that harm our bodies, rather than nurture our existence.

If we function on an information only level, the other parts of us, that perceive on a deeper level, are still operating, we just aren't aware or connected to them. The illusion in its manifestation becomes what many of us have come to orchestrate in our environment and relationships in order to keep our perceptions true for us. To orchestrate what is around us suggests we know what we are doing, which may not be the case, because we are functioning from the subconscious without even recognizing what guidance we have adopted. Our orchestration of events is a product of the compensations we have made internally, in order to preserve our comfort level, and in turn the collective belief about our integrity, within a situation. We have found a way to keep functioning that works to get our needs met on the subconscious level because it is too uncomfortable to build relationship with True Self, and Soul. All the unconscious compensations, and denied emotions, separate us from the ability to know our True Self and Soul. The subconscious is operating out of control because we don't recognize what we have allowed to overcome us, in our absence from attending to the deeper needs of our Soul.

Where exactly does that emotional energy go if we don't allow the experiencing of it? Do we push it down, or stash it somewhere in hopes it will disappear, so we have the illusion of clarity and control over our Self and the environment? After awhile, the emotional component of our being becomes very congested and it is as if it just stops feeling. A numbness and resolve to withdraw from our feelings ensues. We function in our intellect to justify staying where we are. When the emotions nudge towards the surface we really don't want to listen to them because there looms the threat that it may consume us, or reduce us to a state of defeat and out of control of ourselves. Our state of disease, the aspect of Self unrealized in its fullness, will find a way to express its Self, whether it is through our mentality, our emotions, or through the development of symptoms in the physical body. We can consciously choose how we wish to accept our challenges, the things that make us uncomfortable, so that they become opportunities for growth, rather than ultimately becoming a threat to our survival. To cultivate honesty with our Self, and others, about the way we really think and feel about things in the present, is to bring what we don't recognize in our limited perceptions, out into the open. When an illusion is revealed, it is hard to believe we functioned with it so unknowingly for so long. It is completely sobering, for in that moment of realization, we are left initially without any reference for who we really are. Our delusion is as clear as day when we do see it, and it is impossible to recreate the illusion, without completely betraying our integrity with our Soul.

BODY SENSATION

The level of perceiving body sensation represents the physical expression of the unconscious mind. It is just beyond the perception of the illusion, so there is no current understanding of what is being expressed by the unconscious mind. The sensations are the feelings such as rising, falling, sinking, relaxing, expanding, fullness, and emptiness experienced by the mind/body. To perceive through sensation is to experience through the feeling of the experience, as the body and mind have experienced it. The sensation reveals a new awareness that takes us past the illusion, and places us next to the reality of what the *perception of energy* can reveal. When perceiving at the sensation level, we have little interest in what something is called, and the facts that support it. The experience of the sensation puts us in touch with what something really is. This is a much closer expression of truth within ourselves, as it leaves behind the common beliefs that have previously defined it for us. Ego and logic get left behind as this level is entered with the intent of unveiling the truth of the experience as it is held in the cell memory. The sensation represents the realization that there is more to what we are responding to, then we currently know, or have reference for on the conscious level.

ENERGY

To perceive on the energetic level is to become the state of the experience. Children are excellent examples of perceiving on the energetic level. Physically and mentally and emotionally they resonate with energy patterns, lights and sounds. With their whole being they perceive and respond to the energy of their environment without *thinking* about it. There is little interest in the name or facts about the experience, it just is. If you put a young child in a room with music, within minutes they are moving with the music. If it is dance music with lots of rhythm their movement will reflect the Essence of that music and they will be jumping around or stomping their feet. If the music is like a lullaby they will become soft and relaxed reflecting a dreamlike state. In this state of perception the boundaries between the external and the internal begin to dissipate.

In experiencing the sensation level of perception we are given a tool that when we bring our focus to the sensation, and allow ourselves to enter fully into experiencing the sensation, we in Essence become the sensation. In this act of consciously becoming immersed in the sensation we have *become* the energy. For an unresolved aspect of Self, this is to become the person we were at the time of the original incident. In becoming them, we leave behind our assumptions and memory of that experience as we have come to remember it, and enter it as if for the first time. We come to know it as it really is, rather than as we may have come to remember it. Going back and experiencing it as if for the first time, we have the ability to perceive more than we did at that time, because we have grown since then. The sensation itself takes us to the original incident through awareness of the subtle energy. We actually become the energy, physically, mentally and emotionally. Through the energy we are transported past the limitation of time and space to the origins of the retained cell memory that is unresolved. In becoming the energy it becomes an experience in the now, no longer in the past, so we are able to experience it with our current tools of understanding rather than our limited experience at the time of its origin.

The cells of our physical body hold the negative energy of unresolved experience, and with it any trapped toxicity, both in their original state at the time of incidence. These same cells from that first experience onwards attract and accumulate similar vibrations in the form of emotions and thoughts that we are resonating with unconsciously. They act as a magnet and draw to themselves their likeness from our environment, similar circumstances and thought patterns in others. Not only do we begin to repeat similar situations as a result of this unrecognized beacon within us, but we also become heavier in vibration as our physical body begins to collect the physical components that resonate with these energies. Every passing day more toxicity becomes trapped by the density of the physical body's energetic and physical accumulations that build up over time within us. We continue to contribute to producing the physical toxicity in our environment because its harmful effect on us has gone unrecognized. We are blind to that which we have unknowingly orchestrated in keeping ourselves feeling comfortable. In remaining unconscious in our experience of life, we are oblivious to the interconnectedness and reciprocity that we have with all life. We remain in the illusion that we are separate and beyond having any personal responsibility or power to change our collective experience here on earth.

By becoming the energy of that encapsulated memory, we have the ability to understand ourselves in a way that gets past what we have come to remember about the initial experience. The cells respond to the energy of being recognized in their truth, by releasing what they have been holding in containment, both on the physical and energetic levels. Think of this in terms of our immune system. If our body functions mirror our state of mind, then to recognize on a mental, and emotional level, that which isolates us, is to reinitiate the body's ability to naturally resolve our state of disease on the physical level as well. Our immune system is directly influenced by our body's ability to operate in openness, and ease, rather than defensively using its resources to defend itself from perceived threats. The less accumulations we have, the less that pulls us into retreat, when we are faced with new situations. To liberate a negative experience into a fuller expression of who we really are will change the way the cell functions and in turn free all that has been encapsulated with it. The body's vibration increases and we naturally begin supporting ideas and actions that resonate with these higher frequencies. We are again brought into alignment with our true state of health and vitality. We become authentically, the goodness that we long to experience, in others, our life, and ourselves.

In becoming the energy, we are able to *be in the place of experiencing our limitation as if for the first time in its original existence.* It is in this energy that we navigate with our extra senses to go to the place of origin of that perception and therefore go beyond the framework of the held perception of our current experience.

Energy knows no time, as it is forever and *now* always. To be in the energy of a memory brings the original experience into the present for us. We become that person again in all senses. The beauty of working with this level of perception is that to go back to a previous trauma, or unresolved event, allows us to initially experience it as we did originally, but then apply our developed understanding of today, to see it in its polarity. We are different people today, than we were when the incidence occurred. We have developed other aspects of Self since that time, so to return to the perceived trauma, we have resources now that we didn't have then, to perceive more of the truth that was present. The aspects of Self already developed, enable us to liberate the one aspect of Self that has been left behind in being actualized. Bringing awareness to energy allows us to go back at a later time, when we do have the resources to understand and assimilate the experience, to integrate the initial experience, into who we are today. Energy acts as a bridge to retrieve the parts of ourselves we have left encapsulated, until we were ready to liberate them from their original limited experience.

We are often reminded to live in the moment. With energy, all that we have come to experience in it's realized form is with us in this moment, to further enrich our current perception of what we are in the moment. In this moment are also the limited perceptions from our past, that filter out what we have not come to realize about ourselves, and they are triggered by our focus in the moment, because as a Soul we want to bring awareness to our Whole experience. To work with energy is to bring the past into the now, so we can, within this very moment, expand our awareness of Self, and in turn realize the depth and meaning of the whole picture we are part of as a Soul, in this moment. There is great potential offered, in realizing our contribution in bringing awareness to our honest perception in the present moment.

Growing up I remember countless late nights of sitting at the kitchen table with my mom drinking tea while we shared ideas, and hypothesized about life and our place in it. We didn't talk about God, we didn't talk about cooking or cleaning or about other people. We talked about how we saw and felt about what was happening in our lives. We seemed to always start out at the opposite ends of the pole with one another in how we saw something, until we got to what we felt inside, in honesty. It took hours sometimes, but we both always felt good in the common understanding we left with. My mom went back to University for her Masters of Divinity when I was twenty and became an Ordained Reverend in the Evangelical Lutheran Church of Canada. She was very involved in her work for the next number of years, and so our kitchen table talks were not as frequent. I've always been an experiential learner because I wanted to simplify what was presented in complex theories into something I could relate to, and in turn live by, through my own understanding. In learning to appreciate my connection with others, I realize that much of what both my parents have shown me, and shared with me, has become the foundation for what I have since gone on to further in myself. This is why I say that I don't believe there is anything original, as it is all our individual expression of the origin. We can be on what appears to be opposite ends of the pole in our perception of the very same thing. Through our honesty with others, we often come to appreciate this diversity, as it offers illumination, of what symbolically is often right in front of us, in it's Essence all along. Those late nights evolved over time, and validated so much of what I have come to realize since then. There is common understanding we can all attain with one another, if we just have faith that everything is as it should be, and catch our assumptions, and expectations of our Self and one another, so we can hear in clarity what another is sharing with us. We just might find our True Self, and humility, in the wake of their truth.

THE SOURCE OF ALL

It is impossible to put adequate words or expression to this level of perception. From this level of consciousness, all the other levels are revealed in their truth, but there is absolutely no attachment to them. The perception is both external and internal at the same time. We are at complete peace with the All of our experience. Assimilating at this level happens on a knowing level, as there is no spoken language that can define or express it in its Wholeness or completeness. When we are able to perceive from this level, initial experiences are hard to remember in their details, as it is the Essence that remains. The experience becomes symbolic. There is understanding on a Being level. The perception of the name, description, emotion, illusion, sensation and energy are not important anymore even though we may have complete knowledge of them; they are no longer the focus. Instead, these levels of perception become mere limitation to perceiving the whole picture in its truth at the level of consciousness. The Source of All is like the vantage of being in Heaven where nothing is good or bad. The veil of what is presented to us is removed and all that remains is the truth of it. The perfection in everything is revealed in its truth. This level of truth, when realized, is the basis for healing. It is here that healing originates because health is our natural state and there remains nothing to separate us from experiencing it.

THE COMPONENTS OF AWARENESS

The Components of Awareness are the flip side of the coin to our current perceptions. To define the levels of perception is helpful in integrating our currently held perception of what we are, with a greater Awareness of our true nature. In creating a structure for our rational mind, we also create a sense of safety to venture into a new realm of perceiving. In the realm of subtle energy, new components reveal themselves to us, that we have little reference for except through our direct experience of them. To feel lost in the wilderness is a very different experience, then setting out to explore new territory with knowledge that you have within you, and around you, everything that you need, at any given moment. Support, and guidance, arrives in the form of subtle energy that our external world quite often can't endorse for us. It becomes important to us on the conscious level to be able to put context to our observations, and sensing of information. Otherwise, we fail to provide clarity for ourselves, and gain confidence in what we perceive intuitively. Re-defining our understanding as we go along helps us to maintain equilibrium between our subtle senses, and our physical senses, during the process of Self Actualization.

This process of integrating what we currently know, with what we experience in its truth, involves changing the way we perceive things. The layers, in which we perceive, in relationship to our Self, rely on the awakening of our awareness to these subtle energies, our intuition. The experience of awakening awareness requires a means to relate to what is being revealed to us. The following descriptions are for the purpose of structuring what is not tangible in our physical reality, as a means to begin working with it. To talk about and share with others what we encounter on the spiritual, emotional, and mental levels is difficult without creating some form of structure that allows us a common language to help describe what has historically been abstract and conceptual in nature. My work is body based, in other words every observation is in relation to the physical body, the emotional body, the mental body or the spiritual body of the individual. Whether we are looking at the whole body, the current life challenge we are experiencing, an area of the body that a particular symptom has manifested, or a single cell, in my experience there is a common sequence in which the layers of awareness present themselves to us, and if each were followed to its depth, they all ultimately reveal the same truth about a particular disease state.

Our mind has the ability to express and make its presence known on all levels of our experience, be it the intellect, the physical body, the emotions, or through our Spirit. So if we are currently experiencing conflict in a primary relationship with another person, it will also be expressed through our mental perceptions, as well as our physical, spiritual and emotional state. The same goes for a physical ailment, it will be creating certain perceptions in the intellect, as well as our spiritual, and emotional state. An emotional experience will also be recognized in the physical, spiritual and mental states. We have intelligence beyond our brains ability to assimilate and make conscious our perceptions. The mind is operating on all levels, whether we are in awareness of it or not, and it will express itself, in all levels of our experience. To experience the minds levels of perception is difficult without becoming integrated with our extra senses that help us to develop Awareness of our True Self within a situation. With the engagement of our intuition, we can come to integrate our mental, emotional, physical, and spiritual bodies, as balanced in their experience of our true being, Soul.

The following are my interpretations of how I perceive, what many have named before me, over the course of human history. We all have our own relationship to these, and I believe we are all limited in our explanation, as it is the realm of possibility, and the abstract, in which they originate for us. There are also some names that I have given to help define specific types of energy patterns that have emerged through this layered journey to our core, for the purpose of explaining my concepts. It may be helpful to receive the following information, not as fact, but as my interpretations, and suspend making any decisions as to its validity, until we explore them further from an experiential vantage point, versus whether it makes sense or not to our intellect. You can change your mind at any time, name them what you like, and adopt your own interpretations from your personal experience in the realm of subtle energy. These are merely observations, and idea's that my intuition and experience has provided for me, to understand what was beyond the parameters of my education in Medicine. Our mind, and more importantly what we choose to consciously bring to our awareness, is probably the only thing we can control. We all have freedom to consciously choose what beliefs and perceptions we adopt, but to entertain the possibilities of what unknowingly we have become, and have to the potential of becoming in awareness, is to have an open mind. All an open mind requires is fostering faith in something that is ultimately within us, our Soul, the aspect of the Divine within.

THE SOUL

This is our individual Aspect of the Divine or our Divine Essence. It is at the level of the Soul that we find the Divine Individuality within each of us. The Soul is our unique expression and experience of the Source of All. From this perspective we are the center of the universe. The Soul, Core Star, or True Self is the most essential nature of our being. It has been who we are since the beginning of time. The Soul carries with it every experience in its Essence that we have had since the inception of time itself. Whether or not you believe in past lives is not important here.

> *What is important to remember*
> *is that our Soul has maintained its integrity through every circumstance*
> *and remains completely pure and untarnished by experience.*
> *The Soul retains the Essence of every experience*
> *and becomes fuller in its knowledge of its potential.*

The Soul is beyond the limitations of time, space and belief. We recognize its voice as that which we have always known ourselves to be since birth. It is expressed through our True Self. In touch with this Essence of ourselves, we are wise, loving, and full of courage and compassion. It is our basic nature, as it is the deepest goodness, within us all. As we come to experience fuller expressions of the aspects of Self, in harmony with our greater truth of Soul, we become closer to the experience of Wholeness. The experience of Wholeness is to live in full knowledge of the beauty, creativity, spontaneity and wonder of the Soul. The Soul is the part of us that shines brightly, and who's light can never be extinguished, for it reaches beyond the physical realm of existence, as we have come to accept it here on earth. Our experience in its Essence, in its truest form, is preserved here and becomes One with the ALL. Our Soul is who we really are in our magnificence. The best thing is that we all have a Soul and we are equally brilliant, though unique in experience and expression, when connected to the truth of who we are, as Soul.

THE SENSITIVITY

Our Sensitivity is what we place between our conscious mind and our Soul. Our Sensitivity is our ability to perceive more than what our physical senses are able to confirm for us. These other receptors for sensing is what allows us to experience something that is revealed on the energetic level that goes beyond what most perceive on the physical level. To sense at this level is to be *Sensitive to subtle energy*, to enter a state of awareness that accentuates our ability to perceive these *invisible* components of reality. Clairsentience, clairaudience, and clairvoyance, are all expressions of our Sensitivity in awareness. Our Sensitivities are our Gifts to be used to facilitate our ability to experience more depth to the current experience of Earth as most perceive it. I refer to this as our Sensitivity to take us away from the preconceived ideas about Psychic abilities. These abilities are present in us all, and can be developed naturally and with reference to something we know the most about, and can learn to trust, our Selves. There is no need to go 'way out there' in order to connect to a greater truth, because we can do it within the safety of our own Temple, our physical bodies.

In the Merriam-Webster Dictionary, psychic is defined as follows:

Etymology: Greek psychikos: of the Soul, from psychE Soul

1: of or relating to the psyche: psychogenic

2: lying outside the sphere of physical science or knowledge: immaterial, moral, or spiritual in origin or force

3: sensitive to nonphysical or supernatural forces and influences: marked by extraordinary or mysterious Sensitivity, Perception, or understanding

In working with body wisdom, which represents our subconscious mind, we find subtle information, including our Sensitivity, on many levels within the cells of our physical body. The Sensitivity commonly submerges on a conscious level, when we encounter situations or find ourselves in circumstance that we are unable to assimilate or cope with. Our Sensitivity in its ability to perceive with extrasensory awareness is often blocked from our experience because of a perception that gets in the way. The perception that creates the greatest challenge when engaged is our emotions. As soon as our emotions become our experience, and we fail to accept them and embrace them as real for us in the moment, we separate from the part of Self that has become engaged and seeks recognition to liberate itself into a fuller expression. With the actualization of an aspect of Self is the Sensitivity that this liberated aspect carries with it. We *think* we are maintaining integrity in the moment by not allowing our emotions to surface, when in reality we are separating ourselves from a full and free experience of who we are in that moment. The aspect of Self, that is unrealized in its completeness, is left isolated, to influence us subconsciously, so we compensate to preserve composure, in what we *choose* to project of our Self in the moment. We will continue to find ourselves in situations that repeatedly attempt to expose this illusion to us, but as long as we allow our emotions to be a threat to our experience, we can never move beyond them, to experience the true meaning of their expression.

Deep inside is our Soul, extending itself as far as it can, to beckon us nearer to its truth, but we can't hear it, or feel it, through the emotions. Our emotions become our greatest deceivers in our denial of them. We are fooled into believing our emotions are who we are in that moment, and in not accepting them as they are being felt by us, we give power to the intellect, which would have us believe, we are not safe to expose our Self. Most of us have come to define this block as our vulnerability. To unconsciously place our focus on our vulnerability, by denying it exists, is to separate us from our internal resources that can pull us past these limited perceptions, to become connected with our greater resources, the Sensitivity. With the Sensitivity we have the ability to unveil a greater truth for ourselves. The emotions are strong, but the power of Soul is infinitely stronger, so when we accept the emotions, and really feel them, we are clearing the path to see our illusion, and in turn, embrace a greater truth within that is yearning to be recognized.

My work is based on aligning ourselves with our positive potential and trusting Spirit, the part of our Mind that has the ability to reveal the path to healing for us. Therefore, I refer to this component as our Sensitivity, even though when we are separated from this awareness in its truth, it appears to us as vulnerability. To hold onto the illusion of vulnerability, is to serve only one purpose- to maintain a false sense of reality for our Self, so we don't have to change the way we are currently experiencing our Self.

From inception to the age of seven is the usual stage of development that the Sensitivity becomes trapped through a traumatic experience, because we are innocent. The child stops expressing, and growing in some aspect of themselves, from this point onwards. Our Sensitivity is the part of us that we became separated from at a certain age or stage of development. From the point of the negative experience that was beyond our ability to comprehend at that time, onwards, we have filtered our perceptions, to endorse what we decided about ourselves or about life in that moment of experiencing separation from love. We knew *at that time* that we had made a decision about how we chose to perceive things from our experience of betrayal, hurt, or abandonment, in that moment, but that decision is long forgotten. What remains is the illusion of vulnerability. Our Sensitivity, used as a vehicle of awareness, allows us to become reunited with the part of Self that we became separated from and liberate it in its fullness to become part of us and in harmony with Soul, in the present.

We have an experience of something that is in complete contradiction to what we know to be the goodness within ourselves, or others, at a certain point in the development of various aspects of Self. The experience of cruelty, betrayal, abandonment, containment of creativity, and feeling misunderstood, or unsafe at some level, be it emotional or physical, falls into this category. The external world has provided an experience that our internal world cannot understand, or make peace with, at a certain time during our development. The negative experience in the circumstance interrupted our ability to assimilate, or see it from a higher truth. What was experienced from a higher truth, unconsciously, was not consciously realized because trauma got in the way. In denial of expression, because as a child we were not safe, an aspect of Self has been stopped in its tracks, from becoming actualized. As adults, we are not dependent on others in the same way for our survival. We have the ability to liberate this stunted aspect of Self through creating trust and honesty within, to feel our emotions again, without shame and without fear of betrayal. Whether we outwardly share our emotions doesn't matter, but to deny their existence within is to betray True Self, which only serves to confirm our limited perception, as it already exists. We co-create with others all the time, so to actualize our potential in a situation, is to maintain integrity to withstand challenge, through placing faith in expanded awareness. Otherwise, we continue through life having the initial experience unknowingly define our experience before we are even present in the current moment. We are not able to be present with the potential to heal, in the current situation, as long as we are responding unconsciously, from the past. Bringing awareness to our Sensitivity can free us to actualize our potential in our current experience because we see it for what it is, and our part becomes clear.

Developing our intuition requires going back and reclaiming these gifts, our Sensitivities, so we can have a fuller experience of our Soul. These unresolved, or left behind pieces of Self, are encapsulated in our bodies, and we surround them with a wall to keep them safe. We create compensations in order to make up for their loss, and we adopt very sophisticated ways in which to function without them. After a time we don't miss the Sensitivity because the memory of the pain, hurt or negative emotion is what we have come to remember, and it serves to keep us separate from our actualized abilities. The Sensitivity, becomes in our perception, our vulnerability, and we go to great lengths to keep not only others, but ourselves away from it, because it is uncomfortable to consciously *think* about. Ironically, because we live in fear of repeating the traumatic experience, we don't realize the amount of focus we place on avoiding similar circumstances. Subconsciously, this fear becomes our repeated reality, as it goes unrealized in its ability to express itself through our unconscious choices. We become what we fear most in ourselves, without even recognizing it as our own doing.

How many of us have said " I never want to be like my father or mother?" and what becomes of us over time? We are telling the truth, as we have consciously chosen to perceive it when we say we are nothing like them. Our fear being that as we mature into adults ourselves, we may repeat the negativity we experienced of them, as children. In maintaining the perception in its original state, we have separated from the knowledge of the fear for so long, that we have forgotten ever having the Sensitivity that became encapsulated with the initial perception. We have in a *sense* become void of the ability to perceive the higher truth through separating from this one Sensitivity. When greater awareness is achieved the higher aspects of another also become revealed to us. No longer do we resonate with the negative expressions of another, but instead we come to appreciate the more spiritual aspects, that we too value as part of ourselves.

It is often the out of the ordinary events we remember from childhood. A mother and a father are more than what we may appreciate in our experience as a child in relationship to them, through isolated incidents. We are born from them so we carry their Essence in its perfection within us. Whether we are connected to the truth of this Essence, and are able to consciously develop it into our own individuality, rests completely with us. So for all the mothers and the fathers in the world that we feel have let us down, it is within our own Self that we expand our awareness, to be able to liberate our Sensitivity, to be able to appreciate all that we are, and in turn feel gratitude for relationship with them, and honor them for their part in our development. To become in awareness, what we most value in them, whether they realized it or not in their lifetime, is the basis of evolution, and the gift of consciousness for us all.

In our current life experience, we have the ability to make this expanded awareness become a living reality for us. The background to the following incident is that my parents divorced when I was twelve. It was those 'table talks' with my mom that went around and around, that led me to seek easier ways to heal our wounds then the endless talk route. That is what we knew though, and it did move me to work intuitively to go to the root of something, beyond my conscious ability to recognize in myself sometimes. Trying to figure out our place in things is impossible, if we are unable separate from the personal experience, and reunite with the truth of our experience that shows us our Oneness. My own divorce appeared very differently than my parents to me, because of how I healed from those nights talking with my mom. It was important to me that my children never thought they were victims of circumstance, or felt betrayed because their idea of family was disrupted. It wasn't about them, but they were part of the situation. I wanted them to see that they were still every bit as wonderful and important to us, even if we couldn't all live together anymore.

When I divorced, my children were both under the age of seven. They didn't really understand what was happening. I remember sitting them down with their father present, and I drew two circles, side by side, on a piece of paper. One circle represented me, and the other was their father. I divided each circle in half, on one side I wrote 'good', and on the other 'bad'. I told them, that their father and me each had half of us that was good, and half that was bad. I explained that when we decided to have children, we agreed that only the good half of each of us would go together to make them. When I drew them each as their own circle beneath us, I filled in both halves with 'good', so they could see that the Whole of them was made up of only the 'good' half of each of us. Therefore, they would always have only the good from each of us with them, whether we were all living together or not. Only we personally can choose how we see ourselves in life circumstance, but it helps if we have those around us when we are children, that endorse the goodness that is inherent in us.

With each generation, and each time a similar situation is experienced, we are each given the opportunity to bring more to it because of how we have grown from our initial experience. If the hurt and emotional charge of the original situation is left unknowingly influencing us, we are disconnected from the very Sensitivity that can guide us towards clarity. Energy knows no time or space, so to follow where it guides us in awareness reveals the origin of separation from our true Sensitivity. It is with our Sensitivity, that we are able to see our role in facilitating Wholeness in others who are dependant on our decisions and actions. When we are true to Soul, there is always an outcome that benefits everyone, even if not realized completely at the time.

UNCONSCIOUS & SUBCONSCIOUS MIND

For the purpose of defining the components of awareness, the unconscious mind, for this body of work will represent in broad terms, everything we don't know about ourselves in its truth, on the conscious level. The active aspects of Self that are creating disharmony that we have no conscious awareness of within our bodies I am referring to as the subconscious mind. The subconscious mind represents the beliefs, the compensations, the way we have *personally* come to function without realizing what we are doing. Subconscious mind to me is the personal information that we are unknowingly influenced by, that is actively engaged within us. Whereas unconscious mind is not only ours, but collective programs that are not actively engaged or specifically resonating with our body energy or current experience. It is not to say that we have no knowledge of what lies in our subconscious or unconscious mind as it effects us everyday, but we have cut ourselves off from working hand in hand with its capabilities and ability to reveal to us in awareness how we are expressing it in our many levels of daily functioning. In the Process of Inner Alchemy we are looking to bring awareness to the subconscious aspects of Self-operating in unconsciousness to transform what no longer serves us into fuller, positive expressions of who we are from the state of awareness. Inner Alchemy in energy terms is about transforming a lower frequency vibration to a higher frequency vibration. In order to do this we have to come to recognize the components we are working with so we have the opportunity to change the perception from the place of origin, which lies in the subconscious mind. The subconscious mind can be our revealer if we learn to work with it constructively and with respect for its ability to reveal itself clearly to us through awareness.

Our physical body is the temple for our Spirit. Our physical body itself is a tangible means to bring awareness to all that directly relates to our personal information on the energetic level of perception. Through the physical state of the body we can trace the energetic connections on all levels of awareness that relate specifically to our unique state of disease as the physical body is currently expressing its Self. In reconnecting with Intuition to heal the Self we use our body as the authority for our disease state. To be guided by the body is to align our awareness with the wisdom it expresses about its Self that we do not recognize is engaged. To bring our awareness to the body is to get past the busy dialogue that consumes most of our heads. It requires listening on a different level because it is like walking into a dark, soundproof room that we have never been in before. We need to get out of our heads and into our hearts to hear truth as the body can express it. Each cell in our body is programmed by our mind and carries our beliefs and perceptions of reality. Where our Spirit goes, the body follows, so our repeated thoughts charged with emotion, engage Spirit to bring that experience into our awareness. We resonate and are drawn to exactly what the Spirit has been directed, consciously or subconsciously, to bring to our awareness. In response to how we experience what is brought into our perceptions we activate programs that the body functions from without necessarily recognizing our subconscious intent. Another way of looking at this is that bringing awareness to what we invest our thoughts and emotions in the most on the conscious level will lead us to where we have unknowingly been programming our Self through unintentional attention. It is not the thoughts and beliefs that we are consciously aware of that create the problems for the functioning of our body. It is the beliefs we don't recognize, or realize we are investing in with our thoughts, that can create the problems, because they may be in contradiction to a chosen belief or value we choose consciously in the present. One aspect of Self is working against itself without us even knowing it and it creates discomfort for us, and ultimately creating symptoms to express the Self's imbalance. The imbalance becomes our state of disease over time if it is not recognized and healed through conscious awareness.

The Soul is at the center of each cell within the body and carries the master program for the human form. It is through the body that we can learn to identify the Sensitivity and be led to the core Essence of the individual. To bring awareness to our Soul is to be able to recognize the programs that are at work subconsciously in contradiction to the beliefs we have chosen consciously to live by. Ultimately, it is our held perception at the level of the Sensitivity that has created the disease state. The Wall has ensured that the Sensitivity in its vulnerable state has been maintained in its separateness, or unawareness, from who we are currently. The Sensitivity does exist in its positive polarity but it is at the level of the Soul that we come to see this in its truth and have the ability to liberate it to reflect who we are in Wholeness in the present.

CONSCIOUS MIND

Conscious mind represents our thoughts, our thinking process, and the great master control for our functioning on the physical, mental, emotional and spiritual levels. It is the component in its multidimensional abilities that overseas and knows all whether we are aware of it or not. To consciously bring awareness to our perceptions is to engage in all aspects of the mind, as it is the meticulous recorder of all the levels of perception and all the experiences we have ever had since the beginning of our existence. To learn about our mind and its many levels of operation is to gain a sense of safety for it is the only thing we have control over. From our conscious thoughts to the many levels of the subconscious, the mind is our information database and link to all within and without the many dimensions of our being. The mind will always protect us and make necessary compensations to maintain its integrity. This act in itself means that there are many things we make decisions about everyday without realizing we have made them. We are constantly giving directions to its functioning through our thoughts. If we feel threatened and don't acknowledge or recognize this as our truth, our mind creates a compensation to maintain our subconscious desire to remain safe and therefore separation from a higher truth is maintained. To work with mind on a conscious level we place our faith in our ability to handle and make decisions that we choose to become our experience through honesty with Self. To disregard mind is to further validate the existence of our duality and take us further from the truth of our Soul. Tapping into our intuitive abilities is to work with our mind's potential as our trusted companion and revealer of our Wholeness and oneness with all.

The conscious mind as a developed component of awareness is to be consciously aware of an aspect of Self as it is being expressed and actively integrating it to be in harmony with Soul where it becomes an expression of True Self. The conscious mind represents everything that we recognize in ourselves, from what we believe, to the choices we make. The conscious mind before our awareness is developed is quite simply the parts of ourselves that we are aware of thinking. It is the busy brain jargon that constantly runs in our heads. This busy brain syndrome is an indication that we are functioning completely separated from the realization of what is going on inside ourselves. All these dialogues that feel like background noise are what keep us from feeling at peace when by ourselves.

A conscious mind unrecognized, is our mind running on subconscious programs. It is a brain that won't shut off, but we have a hard time defining what is going on in it. We aren't aware of half the thoughts we have as our mind carries on dialogues without our awareness, like a white noise. Through the practice of meditation, we learn to quiet the mind, by increasing our awareness of Self. It is the model of meditation that has given me the ability to define and develop the process I have called Inner Alchemy to help integrate the subconscious with the conscious to resolve disease states in individuals. The process was my personal process for some time before I was able to understand what the body does naturally, and put that knowledge into a form that could facilitate others to activate the healer within their being.

SPIRIT

This component of Awareness is often referred to as the Higher Self or Wise Self. The Spirit is the active ethereal part of our being. Our Spirit is multidimensional, beyond the limitations of time and space, and travels and engages with mind and is connected to our Soul. Spirit can be many places at one time for this reason. If we think of the Spirit of God/Goddess, we know that it is not limited to our dimension, to be present in one place at a time, or limited to one expression at a time. Our imagination acts as the doorway to reveal Spirit. Spirit is the ethereal expression of our being. It puts us in contact with our working field for assimilating and perceiving our experience. The working field being the circumstances, events, relationships with people that can best provide for us the means to come to experience in awareness what we have yearned for consciously or unconsciously. It is a greater expression of us than our physical brain, our conscious mind and physical body. Spirit is what bridges our conscious mind and Soul, our Essence. Spirit has the ability to perceive the truth of Soul and integrate this with the perceptions currently held on the conscious level of our thoughts.

Spirit is not a single aspect of Mind. Spirit is multidimensional and it carries the program of the Soul forth. Emotion is what evokes the greatest response from Spirit. Spirit wants us to understand and resolve everything that stands in our way of the experience of Wholeness and Oneness with all. To place a focused intent for healing, with the authentic emotions of honesty with ourselves, is to engage Spirit in actively bringing us closer to all that can facilitate that desire to heal. A sincere prayer to God is to liberate Spirit into action. Spirit will attract all that supports our desire, so we begin to see that it is our mind in one very special aspect at work here. When we place our focus on the intent to heal, what arrives into our conscious awareness often seems to be in contradiction to what our idea of healing is on the conscious level. There is much that is within us that creates our separation from health when we are operating unconsciously.

We engage Spirit every time we think about someone. So, good thoughts and loving thoughts can be blessings if they go to support and encourage faith in another. If there is emotion associated with the thoughts the stronger the directive to Spirit is to deliver the message. When we have an argument with another, and we are thinking constantly about it and wrestling with the situation we are engaged with Spirit. As soon as you placed focus with intent and emotion on that person, you're Spirit went to them. Their Spirit becomes engaged, especially when there is a strong emotional charge of anger and distress that meets it, because it is in direct contact with all aspects of mind. Their mind, specifically the aspect of their Self that becomes triggered, even on the subconscious level, will become active to defend itself. Both parties have the makings of busy brain syndrome going on, in hopes of resolving the conflict. It is no coincidence that several other memories, incidents and related events all come through your thought process as you stew about the argument you had with them. Some of us are completely unaware of this going on but then all of a sudden we feel at peace with that person, or we are in a state of agitation for a few days as the process continues. Often we have a realization or are able to see the situation differently. It no longer bothers us and becomes like a distant memory. Other times we resolve to avoid the circumstance completely as there doesn't feel like there can be resolution and it agitates us to think about it any longer. We choose not to go where Spirit has led us because somewhere within we have subconsciously chosen to keep a safe distance from healing that Sensitivity. A thought, especially if backed by emotion, to Spirit is like an invitation to go out in all directions from our being and find everything that will bring that experience to us to help liberate that aspect of Self that yearns to experience itself more fully. Spirit to me is best expressed through the symbol of the butterfly. To fly on the wings of Spirit in awareness, is to experience freedom in its magnificence, regardless of circumstance.

The Butterfly

Take a thought
and let it go
Open the door
and push it through
to the world of imagination.
-Courage-

Allow it to spread its wings
and take flight
Follow it as the many doors
of possibility emerge
in its light.
-Hope-

Take a breath in this vastness
and allow all the doors to open
Feel your Spirit soar
as the creativity pours
to nourish the Soul.
-Fulfillment-

New thought takes form
which in turn will
experience its cycle
Only to be set free
to find its way home again.
-Faith-

The Process of Inner Achemy

*The Spirit
on the wings of freedom
always leads us
to the truth of the Soul
in its purest form.
-Goodness-*

*Thought transformed
into imagination
changes
the way we perceive life to be
into it's freeform.
-Magnificent-*

-Alison Feather Adams-

COLLECTIVE CONSCIOUSNESS

Collective consciousness is the culmination of what every living thing on this earth has come to realize about their existence on the conscious level of their mind. From the flowers and plants growing in the fields, to the rocks that landscape our environment, to the animals and people that inhabit this planet. This is the expression of the All that we have come to understand about our existence. It is limited to our awareness of Self, as we have come to experience the many aspects of our experience. It is not the Source of ALL; it is only the parts we have come to consciously identify with as common to us all. The Collective Conscious is directly related to the level of perception that has put a Name to the components of our experiences to help identify as a whole what we have agreed is common to all of humanity in our awareness. It represents the limited knowledge of our collective experience, for it is not the ALL, but it is greater than what most of us have come to be aware of in our individual experience on the conscious level.

Collective Consciousness acts as a pool of information of all of our individual experiences as we have come to understand and define them. We are not separate organisms operating independently of one another. We are connected on the level of energy no matter what our current awareness reveals to us. The more we integrate what we come to know of our Soul, and bring forth our Essence in awareness the greater this pool of knowledge becomes for all living things to benefit from. When we talk about a dog, we immediately draw on all that is understood and acknowledged about what a dog is. Whether we are aware of it or not we are influenced and affected by the collective consciousness about dog. It takes courage and faith to discover what is beyond the known facts about dog so it becomes our personal experience and knowledge through discovery.

The same qualities hold true for naming our disease state. To name a disease state such as Multiple Sclerosis is to draw on the collective consciousness about Multiple Sclerosis. The person's individual experience that became the expression of Multiple Sclerosis is bypassed and kept in its encapsulated form within the cells when we are influenced by what is now currently understood and defined collectively as the experience of Multiple Sclerosis. Collective Consciousness placed in context has the ability to move us further in our understanding of our current experience but it is limiting in comparison to the opportunity we all have to come to a greater understanding if we align with Soul. For Soul is our individuality as it exists in relation to the Source of All. Many of us have come to know our Soul, but we are still integrating what we know of ourselves in our Essence with the various aspects of our humanness.

To move, feel and breathe from the level of Soul is to be able to be in ones center all the time, or able to realign more efficiently when pulled out of it. There are always going to be things that take us by surprise and can momentarily, or for a few hours, and possibly days or weeks, take us from our center until we make peace with the experience and become realigned with our True Self again. It seems to me that when we are able to be Soul all the time our human vessel in which to experience ourselves no longer will serve us for we will be fully actualized and in the state of Wholeness and therefore One with All. We will no longer need this vessel in which to come to know ourselves as we will merge once again with the origin. So, I remind myself that to be human is to exercise humility in all that I have to learn and come to accept and heal within myself in all its expressions. For it is my belief that every step we take toward healing the aspects of Self that keep our illusions of separateness alive, we make one more contribution to the collective pool of resources that serves to heal us all. The journey of healing connected to Self is in essence embracing the concept of Selflessness, which brings us to be Soul as the Source within is liberated into its freeform.

To take responsibility for our part of the Whole, in Selfless awareness, is to invest in all of us collectively. The separation between collective consciousness and the Source of All will over time dissolve with this one act of awareness of our contribution as part of it.

INTEGRATING THE LEVELS OF EXPERIENCE

The diagram that follows is a visual representation of the concept of journeying within with the Process of Inner Alchemy. Within the lower dantian, an energy center in the abdomen that is like the womb of the earth, also referred to as the Sea of Qi, resides our Soul. I have placed it low in the abdomen because as we drop through the layers of experience on the journey within, the sensation is that of going down deeper in the body. As our awareness reaches the abdomen, we feel the earth connect with us, and pull our awareness down through the legs to connect with the earth's strength that supports and sustains us. Now, this model is not based on any one philosophy or intended to be an accurate map for actual energy centers, Chinese Medicine or the Chakra system. The most important part of the Process of Inner Alchemy is to be *guided* past what the conscious mind already knows through its existing maps, *to follow the energy*, to bring awareness to a greater truth within. It is through the heart center that we discern the language of the Soul, for it is here that the Spirit is engaged. The purpose of the diagram "Integrating Levels of Experience" is to illustrate the Process of Inner Alchemy so that the concept of engaging an aspect of Self, through the heart center, in line with Soul, can visually be demonstrated.

The trigger point is the energy that most of us readily recognize. It is as it sounds, when we feel antagonized or we react to something external to us such as what someone says to us, does to us, or we witness in our current situation. To bring our attention to the first recognized perception, be it a word that evokes an emotional reaction, a sensation of discomfort within the body, or self-consciousness in a particular situation, this is where the journey of expanded awareness begins. Any one of these we recognize becomes the starting point for an Inner Alchemy Session.

To become familiar with the Levels of Perception is helpful, so it is easier to identify where we are, in context to what we are able to currently sense, and bring into conscious awareness. As soon as we can bring awareness to the fact that we have been triggered we know a distinct signal has been given to us that a specific aspect of Self has been engaged. We all have within us energies that are collectively recognized as aspects but many are working in harmony and do not block us from experiencing our Soul. We also have a number of these aspects that remain dormant until we are operating at a level of consciousness that signals to our subconscious mind that we have the ability to bring a fuller awareness and resolution to an experience of Self that previously was untouchable. So, unless we already have the ability to transform this particular aspect of Self it would not have come into our awareness through the trigger point. Our body's intelligence is phenomenal, and our Spirit and Soul are working towards bringing fulfillment and peace to us through conscious awareness with every moment we are present.

As soon as an aspect of Self is engaged, by learning to bring our attention to what the body is expressing through its energy, we are opened to embrace our Sensitivity, and through an open heart become aligned with Spirit. In awareness of Spirit, we ground to the earth energy, which returns us to the knowledge of True Self. It is through this act of empowerment that we are aligned with the highest of energies from heaven, and the sustenance, and safety, of earth energy, to bring transformation through the levels of the mind, to be united with the physical body. Transformation through the Process of Inner Alchemy is bringing into awareness the positive polarity of the engaged aspect of Self, and going beyond the polarities of Self all together, to see True Self, as we are in our truth. We bring awareness to the occurrence that impressed on us the limited perception that created duality between who we really are as Soul, and who we have come to believe we are, from the impression of our Self in that situation. In liberating this perception of separation we are brought into harmony with our Soul.

When an aspect of Self is actualized in its full spectrum, beyond polarities, it ceases to be engaged and we are free to experience the highest truth of the Soul, through the actualized Self. It is *through* actualized Self that we clearly perceive Soul, for once Self is actualized, it becomes transparent, or in Essence, Selfless. Spirit can freely enter the body, because the aspect of Self that was creating resistance to this higher frequency energy from entering, is now at peace, so an open pathway now exists directly to the Soul.

The Process of Inner Achemy

Integrating the Levels of Experience

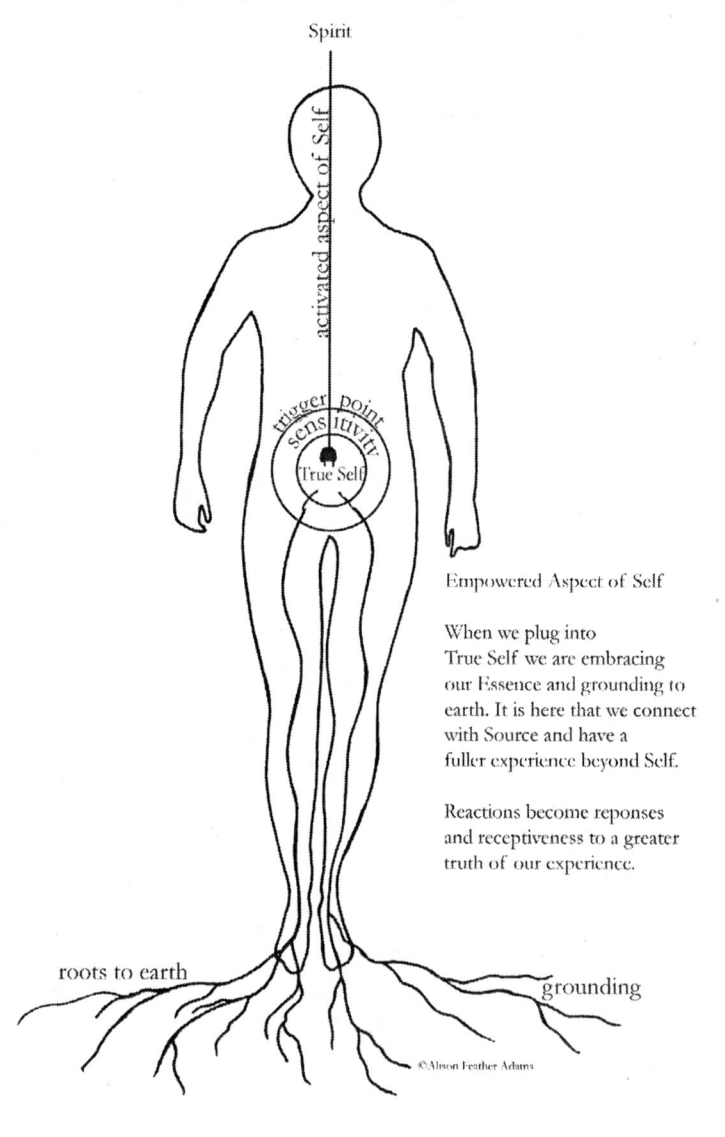

Spirit

activated aspect of Self

trigger point
sensitivity
True Self

Empowered Aspect of Self

When we plug into
True Self we are embracing
our Essence and grounding to
earth. It is here that we connect
with Source and have a
fuller experience beyond Self.

Reactions become reponses
and receptiveness to a greater
truth of our experience.

roots to earth

grounding

©Alison Feather Adams

THE TRIGGER POINT

The trigger point is when we experience a negative reaction to another's words or circumstance we find ourselves in. An external event triggers an internal response that represents a limited perception or belief within ourselves that we do not recognize as being subconscious. In learning to bring awareness to when we are triggered, we can recognize that something external has triggered an unresolved aspect of our Self. The current conscious perception can be the feeling that we have been misunderstood or judged, or it can also be a belief that we hold of another in the situation that requires illumination and understanding on our part. If we experience a negative thought, sensation, or a sudden reaction comes from us towards another we can be sure there is room for growth within an aspect of our Self in some way. Either way, the perception is within us, and the trigger represents our responsibility to recognize a need we have inside ourselves, in order to experience harmony in the situation. What we do recognize is a defensiveness that rears its head in us. The trigger point is a signal that there is more to perceive in the current situation than we are currently aware of because of this hidden unresolved aspect of Self.

Most of us have come to manage this defensiveness with a whole dialogue in our mind that is the loop of justifications and excuses as to why we are innocent. Quite frankly, we can be very clever at creating a whole rationale for remaining exactly the way we are, rather than facing any inadequacy or lack of awareness on our own part. We go to great lengths to keep the cause of our discomfort the responsibility of someone else or the circumstance itself. The wall around the Sensitivity has been approached by another's energy, and our response to them becomes our adopted subconscious compensation for that particular Sensitivity. Once we learn to recognize when we have been triggered, it becomes a signal that we are resonating with a particular pattern of energy that is yearning to be resolved within us. Where there is discomfort, there exists within, the Sensitivity, its polarity as an expression of ease and comfort. In integrating the polarity into our awareness we begin to hear in others what we have been deaf to within ourselves. Not only have we been missing the experience of one of the best parts of our Self, but we have been missing the experience of the best in others as well.

The person who triggered us is really an angel in disguise for they have brought to the forefront that which keeps us separate from recognizing the equal polarity of a positive experience for us. Just because they don't know they are an angel doesn't mean that there is not that aspect of them operating separately from their own conscious awareness. It is still operating even if they don't know it. We miss seeing them with clarity in their light as a result of not recognizing our own aspect of light, as it exists in its truth. If we can come to embrace our own light would it not make sense that we are now in the position to reflect back to them their own light? We hear their words and perceive their actions from our limited internal perception rather than in clarity. This is not to suggest that someone hurting you is all right, but how we respond is completely up to us. Do we engage in the situation from a place of separateness or do we see beyond the illusion of isolation to realize a better outcome for us all?

We all have several aspects of our personality that come forth in various situations. These aspects all have the potential to represent different strengths that are ours to bring forth at will to best serve the situation. To heal the misconceptions and beliefs we hold subconsciously for each of these aspects is to integrate what we really are with the gifts that each of these has the ability to provide for us. We are multidimensional beings with the ability to adapt and integrate many levels of information and experience when we develop the skills to realign with our true Essence, our Soul. These unresolved aspects of ourselves if not fully realized in their potential serve to keep us separate from our Wholeness and keep us from the experience of clarity of who we are in relation to our external world. To remain separate, only serves to isolate us from honestly receiving others, in their current expression of truth. In our clarity, we are able to see beyond the compensations others have adopted, to perceive in awareness their strengths rather than their weakness. If we adopt the mentality of the victim instead of becoming aware of the potential inherent in all life circumstance to bring forth with clarity who we are, we miss the angels that enter our lives. It is very difficult to be clear about our part and recognize the whisper to step forward if we are functioning cut off from our own innate potential.

THE WALL

This level of awareness represents the barrier we encounter where the body has isolated its Sensitivity. The Wall represents the resistance between what we consciously believe our experience to be and our subconsciously held beliefs that we are separate from. When we reach this threshold we are no longer comfortable about continuing, as it is the gateway to the unknown, at least that is the perception from outside of the wall. It feels very big, and impenetrable, and there is a sense of danger and fear that stands guard of it. We hit the wall when we are brought into awareness of the level of sensation. It feels just like a brick wall that we have run into, and we have no reference in our current awareness for what it represents. Notice that the focus of awareness is about *what* it feels like, not *why* it exists. To be guided by the energy of the body we are venturing into new territory in hopes of gaining a better insight into the experience as it has been encapsulated in the body's cells, not as we have come to remember or rewrite it over time. To ask *why* when encountering it is to bring forth our preconceived ideas and everyone else's rather than discovering it, as it exists, within us in our individuality. To encounter the wall is to meet our resistance and something in our perceptions has to shift in order for it to change its form. To bring awareness to sensing the wall and becoming one with the wall through acceptance allows us to enter consciously what we have no known reference for. The Sensitivity at some time in the past has been threatened and in its defense has put up a wall to protect itself. This wall is energetic in origin but the body can create physical boundaries around its state of disease as well. To become aware energetically is to step out of what we know of our disease, into becoming the state of disease in awareness, so we may know it in its truth.

To force our way through the wall is of course possible but it evokes the fight within because it represents a further assault to the original experience of hurt, betrayal and misunderstanding. We are seeking harmony with Self, not further separation. The Sensitivity is not unveiled through force because the mere act of invasion further endorses and engages further compensations and attempts to protect it from our conscious thoughts. To the wall our conscious thoughts and acts of will are a threat. Great stress is placed not only on the physical body, but also the emotional and mental bodies through the act of pushing through the wall to gain access. To forge through is to break open what is contained, and the tools of awareness, our sensitivities necessary to transform what has been encapsulated, are not engaged in conscious awareness. Instead, we are further plummeted into our illusion, and compensations, for we have not acknowledged the state of disease as limited in its expression of our True Self. It remains a threat, and all of our defenses are compromised in resolving it, through the fear of it as disease that has power over us.

As our current beliefs and perceptions exist on the conscious level they are perceived as a threat to the Sensitivity on a subconscious level. Through 'feeling' in awareness we are stepping beyond the limitations the perceived wall has come to recognize as a threat. This wall is indicative of the 'stuck' feeling we reach when journeying within with the

Process of Inner Alchemy, and it is through acceptance that we align ourselves to hearing it in its truth. The Sensitivity as it is within the wall has always remained connected to a higher truth and can only be embraced by an open mind that is resonating with the Soul to gain access. To resonate with Soul, we must be completely present with the Sensation and Energy to know it for what it is in full consciousness.

THE COMPENSATION

We are very clever beings indeed. We make decisions and beliefs about ourselves, consciously in the moment, charged with emotion, based on an experience we perceive as threatening, and then go about life operating from those decisions without remembering having made them. It is as if we trick ourselves into believing the part of our Self that is left functioning with the limited perception of a past event. We subconsciously filter out anything that would show us a different outcome than our previous experience demonstrated to us. In maintaining our perception we recreate the same experience again and again with the outcome predetermined by our held limitation of our Self. For a childhood experience, this makes perfect sense, if we consider that in our innocence, we are completely reliant on others for our safety and needs on all levels. We are dependant as children on our environment to provide safety and comfort for our essential needs on the physical and emotional levels. The threatened part of Self develops compensation, or a way of coping, to survive intact within our environment. The other aspects of our Self, out of necessity to survive, figure out ways to work around this perceived "vulnerable aspect," and compensate for the absence of that one part of Self that experienced hurt or trauma that jeopardized its safety and trust. After awhile this happens without us even being aware of it. At some point that one part that got left behind, retaining the experience as it was at the time of its happening, needs to be retrieved in order to move ahead in our development. It surfaces as a discomfort whenever we are reminded of what is missing within us in our current experience. In continuing to be influenced without awareness by our discomfort we continue to avoid the call of Self, and it becomes a manifested symptom of disease, in an attempt to return us to it, to heal what is keeping it separate from our experience of Wholeness. This part of Self is yearning to be liberated in its truth because underneath the illusion of our discomfort with it, we have retained the innate knowledge of our potential to be free of its limitation.

We do this with physical, mental and emotional wounds. With our physical wounds, to protect ourselves from experiencing further pain, we naturally compensate with our physical structure to alleviate pressure and discomfort. We make compensations on the mental level to protect our Sensitivity and keep ourselves safe from perceived threats and situations with people that make us feel inadequate. The further we advance in our understanding of the aspects of Self the more difficult it becomes to continue the compensations adopted out of necessity at an earlier time. To revisit the decisions that no longer serve us is difficult to do if we don't recognize or remember committing to such decisions. We unconsciously are making choices every moment, so it is natural that not all of them will be in line with a positive perception. Long after a physical injury has healed we can still carry on making physical compensations to protect the original trauma, without even realizing it. The body has maintained the memory of the pain and is still adopting the compensation in response to it. Somewhere the healing was interrupted and the memory was walled off to continue functioning as if 'frozen in time'. To the walled off state of dis- EASE the injury is still in the NOW because it is isolated from knowing how the situation has changed.

The initial compensation, or decision to make adjustments to our existing way of functioning and perceiving ourselves, is locked up somewhere within us, and with it exists the polarity, which is our isolated Sensitivity. This Sensitivity in order to be actualized must be liberated from within the wall, where it too has become stunted in its development. At some point we need to actualize the positive potential in order to have a fuller, more complete experience of True Self. As long as these expressions of Self are contained they are unable to be integrated into our conscious state of awareness, and we go about our daily lives being influenced by our limited perceptions and yet not able to recognize or relate to their origin. We have the ability to develop very complex maneuvers to divert ourselves from coming to face these locked up decisions and beliefs about ourselves in their truth. In an attempt to control all that is exterior to create comfort for ourselves, we avoid confronting the part within that is uncomfortable, and yet can't be identified as tangible. It is a perception, and as such we don't trust it because it is beyond logic as we have come to remember and know the initial experience to be.

We can't change the original circumstance that was harmful to us on the emotional, physical or mental level, but we can update our understanding and perception of it. Through the engagement of intuition we can revisit the original circumstance, see in truth our part in it and the decision we made to protect our Self at that time. If we take the emotional charge out of the situation we come to see it in perspective as if from the vantage point of Heaven. To update the decision to better serve us in the present is much easier to do when we can draw on our other developed resources of strength and clear perception. Ultimately, we are the only ones that can acknowledge our choices and choose to change them into something that better serves our higher good and state of health. A decision made as a child that served to protect us at that time, can become a liability later on when we are in a different circumstance where we are safe. We need that part that was isolated to become part of us again in order to experience Wholeness.

When we recognize that something doesn't feel right or we hear ourselves complaining and become critical of others, it is a good signal that we are not aligned with our own truth. We may be carrying a perception that isn't serving us in the experience of being true to our selves and we will initiate very complex compensations in order to keep it in tact so we can continue functioning feeling justified to remain as we are. Our mind, through our intuition, has the ability to take us to what needs healing within if we place integrity back with our internal state of awareness. We come to identify our needs in the situation in honesty with our Self. Our Mind begins to show us truth rather than deception if we are committed to being honest with ourselves on all levels of perception and with what we are currently experiencing.

ACKNOWLEDGING EMOTION CAN REVEAL OUR ILLUSION

Our emotions can be our greatest ally when we are clear with them, but when they build up unrecognized they can be our greatest deceiver because we don't trust them or know how to relate to them. The suppression of emotion allows us to stay committed to a truth that serves to justify where we are. If acknowledged, our emotions have the ability to take us past our current perceptions to a greater truth and experience of our Self.

I think the experience of our suppressed emotions is akin to a child waking to believe there are monsters in the closet. Imagine you're two years old and you wake up in a dark room and hear something. The shadows take on the shape of scary images. Your imagination goes wild, and you actually conjure up the most horrible thing that lurches in the closet that is going to get you. Your heart races and every part of you feels constricted and unable to move. You have a hard time expressing the great danger you feel closing in on you. Your mother comes in and tries to tell you that there is nothing to fear; it is just your imagination. As a two year old there is faith in your mother because you know she will protect you and wouldn't let anything hurt you. Of course, her words help settle you, but there is still the matter of what lurks in the closet. Our fears can make any dark room ominous and overwhelming. The possibilities flourish as we collect the facts and put together everything that supports our fear. That monster is REAL to us! Thank goodness that mom's are brave and courageous in the eyes of a two year old though, and pretty swift when it comes to comforting their children, but the feeling of fear cannot be consoled by mere words or reasoning in the middle of the night. On goes the light and the search begins. Of course, mom leads in unveiling this horrible monster. The flashlight is turned on and every dark corner is explored.

Then, there is the dreaded closet. At two we haven't yet learned to hold back in expressing our fears. Clinging to mom's leg begging her to just take you from the room into the safety of her bed seems the only sensible thing. After all, if mom opens those closet doors a monster will be unleashed. Mom seems unmoved though, as if she can't see or hear what is right there threatening you. Notice, Mom's holding Sacred Space here because she hasn't bought into your state of perception, she is willing to investigate it with you so you can find out for yourself whether or not your fears are founded! So the quest across the room to the closet is inevitable. Mom opens the doors and shines the light in. Nothing happens! No monster comes roaring out. Parting the clothes and shuffling the contents around there is nothing there. You're right in there with her now looking for some clue to what you had conjured in your mind's eye. It's like it disappeared into thin air what was so real just a moment ago. So, there in the middle of the night the monster is revealed to be but an illusion. With the fear and illusion dispelled, you are left wondering just what was it that created the disturbance? You then discover that the moving shadows are traced to the trees blowing outside and the sounds are heard in clarity now as the breeze blowing through the window screen. The other facts that support comfort and safety now become visible and very settling. So now having taken away the threat of absolute peril it is much easier to see what had evoked the imagination to create such a scenario.

At two it is much easier to dispel our illusions because our emotions are freely expressed and we haven't yet learned to hide our fears from others. An adult has the ability to help us to shine a light where we see darkness and are afraid. At two we have faith and trust in our parents because they are what we have known and relied on to meet our needs so we don't hesitate exposing and expressing our fears to them. We haven't yet developed the Aspects of Self that define us as separate from them yet. It is in the act of openly expressing how we see things that others can help shine a light on our limited perceptions by helping us discover the truth of our perceptions. This requires trust in our sameness at our core level, and as adults we have forgotten this truth, so we are not always in situations that we feel safe to do this. Our fears when expressed to another can be very similar to feeling two again and being caught in an illusion that is real to us, but we know is not serving us. We hesitate exposing our limited Self because we fear the part within that is already isolated may serve to further distance us from others. If we go back to the premise that within us all is goodness and grace and we come forth honestly and courageously to speak our truth is it possible our goodness will be revealed? With this goodness is grace for we have reconnected with innocence again. There is nothing to hide except our courage to be who we are honestly.

As we mature we come to see our parents and respected elders in their humanness and so begins the dissolving of our illusions that they can make everything all right for us all of the time. With the development of our sense of Self we start learning to take responsibility for ourselves and developing courage to face the monsters in the closet alone having faith in a good outcome.

In a perfect childhood this process of becoming harmonious aspects of Self with Soul is a natural evolution, but how many of us had parents who were always patient and always had the time to search with us for monsters in the middle of the night until they were sure that our fears were resolved? That's a pretty tall order for anyone to fill all of the time. So we see adults making compensations for that lack of time and patience required. Concessions are made to help fill that void, because a child's needs on the emotional level are often difficult to understand without the time and patience to listen to them. We have to hear children by being present with them, watching and receiving them through their many expressions as they grow into themselves.

How many of us as children never really learned to face our fears in a positive way? We learned very clever ways to conceal them and appear brave to get our needs met. As adults we don't even remember making these decisions earlier in our life to conceal our true feelings of hurt or betrayal, and the compensations have become our normal operating mode. We have come to expect certain outcomes with relationships and situations before even experiencing them. We don't even recognize these deceptions in ourselves anymore and our relationships are very finely worked out dances that keep them in tact for us. What a mess we create for ourselves and without really knowing the steps we took to bring us to the current experience. No wonder we've become such complex beings with so many problems that seem overwhelming. The saying "we are our worst enemy" comes to mind for me here! Getting past our adopted "fragile" selves takes courage, but there is hope of becoming "real" again if we realize our part in keeping our illusions in place.

THE JOURNEY WITHIN

The following I have identified as the elements of an Inner Alchemy session because they are tangible landmarks for what feels like entering the realm of the unknown. To bring awareness to something we do know or can recognize helps to broaden our currently held perceptions so we can realize a deeper experience in relationship to our Self. The Process of Inner Alchemy is the journey within our being. To understand it with the intellect is to miss the experience of coming to know Self connected to Soul. It is impossible to create a cookbook approach that takes into account the uniqueness of our individual perceptions, but there are common landmarks that we come to recognize once having had the experience of consciously knowing our Soul.

For those that have experienced the depth of a meditative practice that has led to experience of stillness and peace with ALL, than this process will remind them of the same journey. It is through the practice of *Sheng Zhen Wuji Yuan Gong*, a form of Qigong originated by Master Li Jung Fen, that I have come to consciously work with developing the Process of Inner Alchemy that you find here. It has evolved over time as working therapeutically with my patients, following the energy of their body, and being recorder of the body energy for Medical Intuitive Scans has taught me the intelligence of energy beyond my own comprehension. Some part of us is in search for a magic pill that would dissolve all of our illusions, quiet our minds, and bring peace and joy to all of our life experience without any effort. It is maybe in this search for a tangible cure that we have overlooked our own power to heal. I have sought to find a way to help others reach the Essence of their being without getting "stuck" in the negative emotions and trauma of their current experience. More importantly, with serious illness, the threat of the pain inside keeps us isolated from the very power to transform our disease into a state of health again. To find a way to get past the pain so we can experience some relief until we are able to consciously begin healing again, offers a window of hope, when often we are faced with overwhelming odds for survival.

Bringing Spirit into the physical body to me is the unseen power, the invisible magic pill, that we all have access to, that costs nothing on the material plane, and has the ability to transform us on all levels. Inner Alchemy is the process of allowing Spirit to be reunited with our physicality again. It is a method to get past the illusions of our fears, and gain knowledge of the subconscious programs our bodies are running from without our knowledge. Beyond these programs is the power of our Soul that holds our innate potential for healing, waiting to be liberated into action. To heal, without addressing the subconscious programs, is to bring short-term improvement, but reliance on health remains externally enforced, rather than internally validated. We still have to heal the misperceptions and way in which we are living in order to maintain our health. Few can do this unless the perceptions are transformed into awareness of what we are doing to ourselves and in turn our common environment, internally and externally. I have developed the Process of Inner Alchemy to facilitate this process. A sincere desire to be honest with oneself is necessary though. This is very difficult to hear if we are ill because we are overwhelmed, weak and feeling vulnerable. The Process of Inner Alchemy empowers us to take the journey within; in a way we become comfortable enough to rebuild relationship with our healthy state of being. The journey never takes us beyond what we are able to assimilate or handle as we are in complete control of the pace, and depth, in which we allow our perceptions to take us. It is similar to meditation, in that this Process of Inner Alchemy reminds us how to tune into our subtle senses, and learn to hear ourselves in clarity again, through the quietness of the body energy, rather than the busyness of the brain.

The Process of Inner Alchemy begins as a process of unveiling what we have become unknowingly, and becomes a remembering of what we have always been as Soul, but forgotten through the mists of our experience.

THE ELEMENTS OF AN INNER ALCHEMY SESSION

The Breath

Using breath as the initial focus for the Process of Inner Alchemy we are able to bring our awareness into the current expression of the body. It becomes easier to identify our feeling of "stuck" in relation to our physical body when we use breath to feel the resistance as the body is expressing it. The "stuck" perception whether it is mental, emotional or physical in its experience is the inability to move through our current experience with ease. It represents the trigger point when a current experience in the moment evokes a "reaction" from us versus a response from a position of ease. For the Process of Inner Alchemy we require a conscious connection to be made with the energy of the body in its current state of subconscious experience, otherwise an isolated Aspect of our Self remains separate from our Conscious Awareness. Our intuitive sensing on the emotional or sensational levels of perception forms a relationship with the physical body as it is currently expressing its "stuck" perception through energy. There is a need to touch the "stuck" as the body is holding it, in order to understand it, so utilizing the flow of breath through the body enables us to bring focus with the conscious mind to the body's subtle energy. Meditative practices, although unique in their individual techniques, all use breath as a means of bringing focus to the body and to quiet the mind. In this simple act of following breath as it flows through the body we begin the act of attending to the subtle energy the body uses to communicate to us.

The Conscious Mind

Using breath as a guide we are able to bring awareness on the conscious level to the sensation or emotion that is held in its unresolved state, unconsciously within the body. We may not know what these sensations or emotions mean but we have brought them into our awareness. By focusing on the body energy we consciously touch the unknown Aspect of Self that is expressing itself for the first time in context to how the body is holding this Aspect of Self in its original isolated state. The energy being expressed may be one that we recognize but only in context to our current perceptions, not in its state of origin on the subconscious level.

The Spirit

Calling on Spirit with a clear intent to take us to the origin of the imbalance is to engage in what most of us recognize as our imagination. It helps us rise above the trauma, the emotions, and the discomfort to find clarity. It is in the clarity of distance from this particular Aspect of Self that we engage the more developed Aspects of Self and Soul to put in perspective the original experience. On the wings of Spirit, we can bring the past trauma into the NOW. Conscious mind is right there with us on this journey and able to recognize the decision about ones Self or our life made at that time that no longer serves Self in its actualization in the present. Spirit acts as the great liberator in the Process of Inner Alchemy as it represents all Aspects of Self in relation to our Soul.

Consciousness Expanded

To become Consciously Aware of our truth as it was perceived at the time of the trauma, and the Greater Truth, held by the Soul, as it is perceived on the wings of Spirit in clarity is where the journey within takes us. To choose to embrace what no longer serves us in its perception as our vulnerability, and in turn embrace the part of our Self in its Sensitivity is to utilize the perception of Conscious Awareness and empower our Self to work in harmony with our Soul. We are given the opportunity to recognize and re-choose in Conscious Awareness, the decisions and perceptions that support Self in the experience we desire in fulfilling our Soul's purpose. Consciousness means we are in full awareness of our perceptions on the conscious level. We know what we perceive as it is in awareness that we are connected to our thoughts and feelings in the moment.

The Physical Body

The process of attending to the wisdom found in our body takes us past the "stuck" we experience to be aligned with our Center again. It is here we can experience Truth on its many levels and it becomes natural to forgive because in the realization of Truth, there is nothing to forgive. Truth realizes the many expressions of love, including, hurt, jealousy, hatred and anger. How can we not forgive what we understand in its truth, as its expression is no longer threatening *our* ability to be whole? All that remains is the ability to feel love for Self, and in turn the ability to perceive all that is love in others. The feeling is like coming home after being away for a long time from loved ones. It is through the body sensations and energy that is the body's way of communicating through subtle energy, that we come to release the aspect of Self that has been left isolated within us. This aspect of Self in its limited perception and held belief, unless realized, creates discomfort with our True Self and will find a way to express itself, first through the energy of thoughts and emotions, then through the development of symptoms that can be physically recognized.

The Spirit Embodied

To heal, our Spirit must come into our physical body. In the awareness of feeling love for ones Self the physical body is open to receive love from all the unseen forces of our existence. Love has the ability to transform all that is negative and destructive to us, into the nurturing of positive experience. Our physical, mental and emotional bodies become aligned in awareness with all that supports health and healing of the physical, mental and emotional bodies. In this awareness we resonate on all levels with the higher frequencies that draw positive experience to us.

When we release consciously, a subconsciously held perception that only serves to impoverish us, we open ourselves to all that does sustain, nurture and inspire us to be who we really are, connected to Soul. The physical body on the energetic level is now aligned with higher frequency experiences such as joy, peace and love.

The Spirit at Work with Mind & Body

With a sincere intent to heal placed with Spirit, the one Aspect of Self that was held back in the past in its limited perception is set free. A catch up on all levels of experience takes place. That one Aspect had many subtle ties to many events and also shaped the development of perceptions about Self from the time of the original experience. Many body functions and perceptions of other experiences following the original event have been tainted by that initial event, so there are a series of shifts in perceptions that continue to come into our awareness following the session. Spirit has the ability to reconnect us to all that belongs with us, that serves realizing our positive potential, if we place our intent to work with it in its freeform. That missing piece of Self has kept us disconnected from many other levels of awareness that are needed to become whole. For people with serious pathologies, support on the physical level is needed to facilitate the body's ability to discard the toxic accumulations that are released through this energetic process of transformation.

Gratitude

A thought fed by fear manifests disease on one end of the spectrum of health, while the heart filled with gratitude brings ease on the other end of the same spectrum.

Self-love, Self-forgiveness, any acknowledgement of True Self, in honesty, is a form of gratitude. We recognize gratitude when we are moved within by all that we become aware of in others contributions to our growth and experience of joy. We come to recognize the Angels in everyone when we feel gratitude in our heart. A heart filled with gratitude is an open heart that is able to receive Love, and Love is the greatest healer of all.

Gratitude is natural when we come to know ourselves in a new state of awareness because we recognize we have changed, and we realize it didn't happen alone because we are no longer held in the illusion of separation. We acknowledge our own part in facilitating growth, and also the part of others to facilitate our growth. We appreciate all those that dared to be the Angels to us, without being recognized by us, because they loved and believed in us unconditionally. Even the Angels that appeared to us as our enemies are revealed to be a reflection of our own separation from Soul. Those people that hurt us, the Angels in disguise, on the level of their Soul recognized what we had to heal within our Self and they played their part whether they knew it or not in that moment. It is in our healing we come to see a higher truth to our previously held perceptions of others, and we feel gratitude for their part in our actualization. Gratitude is authentic and naturally flowing... it just starts when we connect to the Truth of our Soul because it is a natural stream of expression flowing from Love. Through gratitude we return once again to the realization and experience of Love.

A GUIDE TO AN INNER ALCHEMY SESSION

This is a guide to take you to the state of disease as it exists on the energetic level in relation to the physical body. It is important that if you are currently experiencing a specific symptom that you don't automatically assume this is the area of the body that you will be drawn to when doing this exercise. Please follow the directions as they are given and don't try and bring more into the process than is necessary. At the end of the process you will be able to assimilate and bring further awareness to the initial experience very naturally through the experience of your life and Self in the following few days.

The idea is to go beyond the current perception of the disease state to experience the truth of the imbalance, as it exists in its original state at the cellular level. To begin with no expectations of how this process will be experienced and what it represents is to take the most important step. Be courageous enough to sit in the seat of knowing nothing and you may be very surprised at the wisdom the body is able to convey through its energy if you just attend to what is being expressed and open to receive it in its truth. Your mind will facilitate what is safe and within your grasp to become aware of so there is absolutely no danger in placing faith in this greater aspect of yourself. Trust yourself and you will be guided to liberate the perceptions and beliefs that are subconsciously influencing and limiting your current awareness of Soul.

Begin by placing a sincere intent to hold Sacred Space for your Self. In other words, be honest with your Self, as difficult as it may seem to face the way you really feel, honesty is the one virtue that is going to keep you headed in the right direction towards a greater Truth for your Self in line with your Soul. Choose a place that you are relaxed and feel safe to tune out from your current environment for a few moments. Begin by lying down on your back and bringing your focus to your body against the ground.

AN INNER ALCHEMY SESSION

Bring in the Breath

Imagine you are breathing in through the top of your head and as you exhale follow your breath at is descends down through your body. Just breath naturally, and follow your breath just noticing how it feels as it flows down through your body as you exhale. As you become more relaxed it becomes easier to feel your body respond to the flow of breath descending down through it.

Notice where in your body the breath doesn't want to flow freely through. Just notice where it seems to stop moving down inside your body.

Introduce Conscious Mind to Subconscious Mind

Notice the place in your body where the breath meets resistance in its path from smoothly flowing in through the top of your head and down to your toes. Bring your full attention to this "stuck" feeling in your body. Just feel it. Be with this area in your body for a moment and just accept what it feels like there. Is there an emotion you become aware of there? Or is it a sensation that is present?

Give yourself permission to just accept that feeling and really feel it, even if you can't recognize it as yours, identify with it, or articulate what the exact feeling is. Give yourself permission to just be with it and really feel it.

You may recognize this feeling but not have exact reference for it. Surrender to it so it is able to fully express itself as it is in the NOW.

Introduce Imagination

From the feeling in your body right now, I'd like you to place faith in your subconscious mind to take you to the main event or circumstance that this feeling originated. Your mind knows exactly where to take you if you trust it to guide you to the place of origin in your past.

Imagine you float way up into the clouds above the earth. Look down at the earth surface, far below you. A line will appear running across the earth's surface. This line represents your life, and it stretches from the beginning of time, to way out into eternity. Your mind has recorded meticulously every event that you have ever experienced on all levels of awareness, even what you don't remember through your conscious experience. Let's trust your Spirit, the part of mind that wants you to heal and will guide you back to the exact moment that this feeling originated.

Staying way up above the line you see, ask yourself if the moment in time this feeling originated was before birth, during birth, or after birth. Just take the answer that first comes to you without worrying if it makes sense. Just receive the answer; whether it comes in a "knowing" or a clear answer you hear in your head.

Now completely surrender to Spirit guiding you back along the line far below you to be directly above the place where the experience happened. Stay up above it knowing that directly below you is you in another time having an experience that exists in its original state.

Go down and become you at that time. In this moment you are like another person in that you may not recognize the feelings that you begin experiencing. Be with your body, your thoughts, and your emotions and know they are you at this place of the original experience.

With this feeling filling every part of your body, imagine you have BECOME the feeling.

In this moment you have to figure out where you are by what you do know IN this feeling.

Ask yourself how old you are in this feeling?

Feel your emotions. Feel your body sensations. Notice your breath. Is it more difficult to breathe? Notice your heart rate. Is it relaxed or has it sped up?

In your minds eye, imagine you are looking down at your feet and notice what you are wearing on them. And then bring into your awareness the ground you are standing on.

Fill in the surroundings of this vision starting with the image of your feet.

As you bring focus to the details the clearer the details will appear.

It will feel foreign yet familiar at the same time. Trust what your body is experiencing to guide you.

Just take what information comes to you from the experience of being IN this feeling.

Are you a man, woman, child, or infant?

Feel a sense of what you are in this moment. All your senses, feelings, and thoughts that are your present experience right now as you lie here, are you in this original situation.

Are you in another time? Or do you recognize the place and people you stand in the midst of? In this moment you have entered it as if for the first time. Even if you recognize the event be this person in their experience, not what you think they would experience.

Be that person, in how they perceive and experience their circumstance at that time. Take a few moments to acclimatize to being this person in the way they are, and what is going on in that situation for them. Become them fully. Notice how your body feels like it belongs to someone else? You are a different person in this moment.

What is happening for you in this situation?

Is there a significant event or sense of something happening that is uncomfortable for you?

Remember, if it is a memory you already know about, feel yourself at that time, not what you have retained in your memory of the experience or believed about it before this moment.

Be in the seat of knowing nothing except what is being experienced in this moment through the feelings and sensations you are experiencing right now. This is just energy so there is nothing that can hurt you or be of real threat.

Allow the sensation of the experience to lead you to the truth of your experience as it was for you in that moment.

Introduce New Level of Consciousness

In that moment, through your eyes at that time, what was the decision you made about yourself or your life in the middle of that experience?

Be completely honest here, as this decision was made at another time in the middle of the experience, not now with your current knowledge or understanding of yourself or your life.

Be completely honest about how you feel about yourself in this experience.

To transform the negative charge of the experience into something positive you can perceive, let's create some distance for a few moments.

Imagine you rise up high into the sky, way up into the clouds. You can see yourself at that time as a tiny dot down below you on the ground. There is no detail or feeling here of that person down below, it is as if they are someone now separate from you.

Open the Door for Spirit

Place a sincere intent to heal this part of Self that has had this experience.

We can't change the experience itself, but we can change the effect it has on your current perceptions of experience.

Your Spirit becomes your greatest guide here, as it knows exactly where to take you to reclaim something that belongs with you now, and is needed to move forward in your life as a positive experience of yourself.

Imagine that you are suspended up above the original incident, way up in the clouds and Spirit comes and guides you back, way back to at least an hour before any of the events that led up to that initial experience. Allow yourself to be guided back in time. You don't need to do anything except to be guided.

When you feel you are brought to a stop suspended above in a clear opening, stay there.

Notice that there are no emotions here.

There is a feeling of weightlessness and freedom.

You may feel nothingness in thought or feeling. Feel your body in this sense of calm and freedom. Allow yourself to feel suspended here, as if you are in heaven.

Feelings are excellent beacons that unactualized experiences leave behind as markers for you to find them when you are ready and have the resources cultivated to see them another way.

Did you wonder why this exact circumstance is the one that popped up today out of numerous other ones? There is significance.

There is some part of Self that needs to be realized in awareness for you to move forward towards Wholeness in your current life.

What consciously you have preserved as your vulnerability has its polarity in the form of a Sensitivity waiting to be unveiled. You need that Sensitivity actively working with you now in order to move forward in your life. Living without it is becoming more and more difficult.

Spirit wants nothing more than to reunite you with the level of your Soul so it is willing to guide and expose what you are ready to receive now. This Sensitivity belongs with you now so you can experience Wholeness. That unrealized aspect of Self is creating the experience of separation between you and your Soul. This separation is an illusion, nothing more. To identify and free that encapsulated part of your Self is to free your perceptions in both their negative and positive polarities. In freedom from the limited perception, you are realigned with your potential, where you shine connected to the Truth of your Soul.

The negative feelings have served as beacons to bring you back to this event. Now in recognizing what impression you have retained about yourself, the negative feelings are no longer held in isolation. You've embraced them, acknowledged them, and now they are being released from your body in their freeform. Visualize them dissipating from your body. Notice where from your body this negative energy comes from. In your mind's eye just observe this energy leaving your physical structure. There is nothing to hold these emotions imprisoned within your body anymore. From this vantage of way up in the clouds above earth, feel the lightness to your body now.

Introduce Awareness to Sensitive Self

In this place of peace and freedom there is nothing separating you from bringing to consciousness all the positive virtues present from the initial experience. Bring them into your body and allow them to flow where they need to go. Just witness this process and create a visual to having them become part of you. If you don't know what the virtues are at this moment, that is all right, just know they are now part of you and will become part of your consciousness, as they are now part of you in awareness. Trust these virtues are going to be where they best serve your highest good and they will be completely available to you because now they are part of you in their positive polarity, not separate from your conscious experience.

Experience the Original Situation for What it is at this New Level of Awareness.

There are always both polarities present in every situation. The negative and the positive are always there. Let's go back now to the original event we started out with today, and become who you were there again.

Know that in this moment you are that person in that moment again. Become them.

Are there any negative feelings there now? If there are, thank them for guiding you, and ask that they transform, as they no longer serve you in their present state. There is something else you need to embrace in that situation in order for the negativity to transform to reveal its positive polarity.

Ask that in their place you accept whatever Sensitivity or virtue that is still not integrated with who you really are.

Allow the Sensitivity to be reunited with you now to serve your highest good. Visualize this positive energy coming into your body and becoming part of you. Just observe through your mind's eye where this energy goes.

Embracing the Blessing

The original situation has not changed, but the emotional charge has been neutralized. It is much easier to see the whole truth of it now.

Does the situation feel personally about you now?

While remaining focused on this situation, notice you haven't changed the actual event. What happened hasn't become all right or others parts in it are not justified. All you have done is take the negative emotional charge or the uncomfortable sensation out of your experience so you can see it for what it is without attachment. The situation hasn't changed, but your ability to move beyond the limited experience it provided at that time has changed. This situation no longer serves to separate you from what you are able to actualize in your Self any longer.

Float up above your body as you are in that event and become the observer.

From this perspective what other strength or skill did you discover in yourself as a result of being placed in that situation?

Would you have come to find this strength in yourself if this challenge had not been presented in this way to you? Be honest with yourself.

Whether you were consciously aware of it or not at that time, do you see now looking as the observer what opportunity or gift that event provided for you to realize about some part of your Self?

Now look at that part of your Self, as a separate person than who you are today, and make eye contact with them. Look deeply into their eyes. Is there anything that person needs you to acknowledge in them? Imagine their true needs are being communicated to you and you know exactly what they are asking of you. Really feel them connect with you and keep eye contact with them as they receive it from you.

How does this make you feel in this moment?

How do they appear to you now?

Float up really high into the heavens and see that event fade away as the ground becomes farther and farther away. As you travel back through the heavens to the present time ask that any events or circumstances that had any resonance to that initial experience, that have any negative emotions or attachment, be realized in their positive polarity.

All the positive experience from each one of those life events can now become part of your conscious awareness of who you really are.

With that original perception released in its limitation, what part of other experiences that followed were also perceived with limitation? These particular experiences are now going to be revealed in their positive influence over how you have come to develop yourself.

Now, you are free to accept all the positive polarities of all those experiences that the mind has kept intact for you to receive. Imagine this energy being attracted to you and going right into your body.

Placing this intent with Spirit will make all the connected perceptions shift into the positive polarity that serves your highest good. May all the negatively perceived experiences be revealed in their light and the potential they offered to enrich you from that time of experience forward. Your body is like a magnet that attracts all these positive attributes and gifts that enrich your experience of Self today in alignment with your Soul and the truth of your magnificence. You may have memories come through your mind as you travel back along the line to the present. Just let them pass through your conscious thoughts and know that the mind is assimilating it all in a way that best serves your highest good. The details are not important here; the Essence of the experiences will be part of you to move forward from in the present.

Bring Spirit back to the Physical Body

Float back to the present moment. Come back to be present with your body and feel your connection to the ground you rest on, and the space all around you.

Be with your breath and notice what your body feels like. Take a moment to assimilate all that has happened.

Notice how you feel!!!

Spirit Embodied

Breathe in through the top of your head and follow your breath as it flows through your body now.

Is there any place in your body that it feels like it isn't flowing through smoothly?

Experience Spirit Working with Conscious Mind & Body

If you notice a "stuck" feeling as you bring breath through your body, go to the "stuck" feeling and be with it for a moment.

Really feel it and trust your intuition to tell you what it is asking for you to recognize.

What does that part of you still need?

Just listen with your heart to what comes from within you.

Just let the answer come to you in a knowing.

If you had that one thing, what would it give you?

Be honest with yourself and trust what comes even if it doesn't make sense to you.

Keep asking while holding your focus on the way your body feels.

There will be a positive shift in what your body feels like as soon as you name this for your Self. Your body will feel calm and open as if a great weight has been lifted. When you say the words feel how your body responds to them.

Allow your body energy to guide you in this process.

If a word you bring in gives a feeling of resistance, try another word. When you name it the body will respond and you will feel sure of it. If there is any question in your mind then try another word.

It may surprise you what you have failed to recognize as a need within, up until this moment.

When you have reached this inner truth with your heart you will know it, as it feels like something you have been separated from for a very long time without even knowing it until this minute. The best part of reaching this Truth is the ability to accept it now as something that belongs with you to enrich, nurture, and support your very essence. It is your choice to move forward in the knowledge that this positive acknowledgement is actively present in every part of you. Imagine you have an infinite source of this available to you and all you have to do is breathe it in through the top of your head so it fills you and integrates itself into every aspect of you. Go ahead and imagine it anyway you like, as a color, a sensation, an emotion, however you imagine this thing to be available to you as an infinite source to make you whole.

*Integrating Transformed Aspect of Self
into a Positive Intent that Serves your Highest Good*

Take a moment and imagine a situation in the future, whether it is tomorrow, or next week or a year from now, where you would normally have this stuck feeling we identified today. Imagine yourself in that situation as if it were happening right now.

Are the feelings there or are you thinking them in anticipation? Notice if the actual feelings are there. Do you feel that stuck feeling?

Notice yourself acting and feeling differently. You are moving, expressing yourself, and feeling really good about who you are. Take a snapshot of yourself and how you see yourself. This is a good reminder to give yourself of how you choose to be in your Power. It feels good and notice how others in that situation benefit from experiencing you in this way.

Gratitude

Come back to this present moment and really feel yourself in your body lying on the ground. Take a moment to really enjoy the good feelings you have about yourself and the way you feel right now. The negative feelings are long gone and in their place are positive feelings and perceptions that facilitate experiencing your Self with comfort and ease.

Take a moment to appreciate who you are in this moment and acknowledge the things that you most value in this experience of Self.

Take a moment to reflect back over your life and ask that the Angels that have tried to show this illusion of separation to you, be revealed to you. Those that you had perceived as hurting and isolating you, in the truth of their light, their Soul, had recognized some power within you.

These Angels had trusted you to realize your power through their challenge to an aspect of your Self that needed development. The part of them that acted out of isolation from their True Self, in turn has the potential to be realized by them, by the simple act of you now choosing to stand in your Power from this point forward with them. Choose to be in your Power now so that you may receive the Love that their Soul has for you. May those that appear to be in opposition to who you really are be revealed in their support of you from the level of their Soul.

Watch as the people gather before you in your minds eye that recognized your Power from the level of their Soul. Look in their eyes to receive their truth in this unconditional gift of love to you from their Soul.

When you are ready come back into awareness of your current environment. Take a moment and look around you at all that is beautiful and inspiring that surrounds you.

In this moment you will notice all that reflects and reminds you of your true goodness right there in front of you. Celebrate your connection with it all.

End of Session

The Process of Inner Alchemy can be done anytime you become aware of any uncomfortable feelings either on the emotional or sensational level of experience. To bring the parts of Self that are operating from old programs up to date with the conscious choices you have made for yourself, this process is very valuable to get out of what you think in the present, to bring you back in alignment with the truth of your Soul. To bring past experiences into the NOW in awareness is to transform the subconscious conditioning that separates us from enjoying the gifts being offered to us in the present.

> *Inner Alchemy reveals the gift of clarity*
> *to experience ourselves as we are in Truth,*
> *and to recognize in others, their goodness and grace,*
> *in support of our experience of Wholeness.*
> *Through Inner Alchemy we transform what separates us*
> *from embracing our own goodness and grace,*
> *as it waits patiently to be liberated, from within us.*

In unveiling our Essence, Soul, we enter the truth of Oneness with All.

The Alchemy Frees the Source Within

Our Soul's purpose evades us
when we are cast into the waves of the sea
To be washed over and thrust into the undertow of life
without faith in greatness to embrace us.

Returned to the womb of mother earth herself
without breath, without reverence,
We lose consciousness of her magnificent power
to deliver and guide us.

Surrender and trust in her
to return us again to the shores of understanding
Where our Essence emerges
as being One with her.

Receive the Spirit of grace and gratitude
in the breath of consciousness regained
With the knowledge that we have been awakened
on the shores of change.

Breathe in to receive this blessing in its truth
for it guides us back to our natural state of Oneness
With the sky, sun, moon and earth
in which we recognize our likeness in Essence again.

With Essence illuminated
we may walk with mother earth again
And trust the guidance she offers through all that touches us
in clarity of what we are in this moment with her.

-Alison Feather Adams-

USING INTUITION & INNER ALCHEMY
FOR DAILY PROCESSING

As with all skills, the more we practice using our intuition, the more proficient we become with it. The extra senses become second nature when we have developed and learned to trust what our intuition is revealing to us. To become aware of our extra senses in relation to our everyday experience is much like the experience we had as toddlers learning to use our five physical senses except that as adults we have our conditioned beliefs, values, and life experiences to work through in relation to our natural instincts of intuition. With practice our extra senses are naturally integrated with our external senses and our nervous system begins to adjust to this multi-sensory way of being. To remind our adult Selves to be a Kindergarten student again and enjoy the process, laughing at our misconceptions, playing and meeting new challenges without doubt or fear of being judged as different is really helpful. It takes some practice to integrate our intuitive sensing with common sense as we have come to learn it through our life experience. The teacher is within for interpreting our body signals and ways of assessing information perceived through sensations and consciousness on an energetic level. One really becomes the student when one meets the teacher within. Trust and faith become more firmly rooted in our being as we remind ourselves to "check in" before reaching out.

To apply learned knowledge and information from life experience, with what our bodies can guide us to intuitively as a greater truth of our reality, can take time. Many learned skills can appear as a polarity to our intuitive skills until we come to integrate fully the higher truths of the Soul with what works harmoniously for us as individuals walking our truth on Earth. To become grounded in our bodies is to facilitate the manifestation of the higher truths of the

Soul into current technology and skills to be implemented into our existing physical world. To bring us into harmony with nature and all that supports our health and survival as human beings sharing a common environment with all living things is to empower not only ourselves, but also our shared experience of earth. Intuition adds depth and dimension to the ordinary experiences of everyday and the very act of engaging in life at this multi-sensory level constantly reveals the healing potential of the moment in very unexpected ways.

To begin working with the Process of Inner Alchemy in our daily lives is to notice when we simply don't feel good on the emotional, mental or physical level and bring our reference out of our current thoughts about our discomfort into awareness of our own body energy. If we can remember to follow the energy of how the body responds over what we may think about our current experience, we have the ability to understand and identify the root of our perceptions in relationship to Self. Being guided by energy, in the process of Inner Alchemy, facilitates the shifting of the negative experience into one that liberates a limitation we currently hold subconsciously and reveal its positive polarity that we can move forward from with positive results. We begin to *feel* our way to a greater truth within by engaging our intuitive skills, instead of willing our way through our challenges based on what we think we know. How many times do we want different results without making any changes to the way we are currently doing things? It doesn't make sense but this is what it seems to boil down to sometimes for many of us. Bringing the integrity back to our Self with honesty makes our daily decisions become choices made in Awareness rather than unconsciously or by default.

The beauty of working with energy for this process of transformation is that energy can always be in the Now. Making a mental note of the times during the day that we feel uncomfortable, or triggered, by either by an incident, an exchange with another person, or a perception we had in passing, gives us a marker for later processing. These very incidents can be brought forward into the Now when we have the time to spend being with the feeling and attending to the energy of the body when the thought is revisited in Sacred Space. Even to make a note of some of the incidents that we repeatedly think about, or when we think of them they bother us by either making us agitated or upset just to have them run through our mind. These are markers for places that the Process of Inner Alchemy can take us to transform our hurts into positive learning experiences for the Aspect of Self that was engaged and limited in its perception.

Through humility and honesty we endorse our faith in Self to align with the truth of the Soul so we continue to learn and grow through our daily experiences. There is something extraordinary in all that appears ordinary, but it takes great courage to step into the unknown time and time again from a place of discomfort. Our fears are gradually quieted as we come to embrace the gift of seeing the world through the eyes of innocence and have our intentions begin naturally emerging from the experience of unconditional love. Ultimately, Sense of Self dissolves into the experience of Selflessness as we function on all levels in harmony with Soul.

PART FOUR:
Case Studies

I've included some case studies because it can be helpful to hear how others have courageously journeyed within, to transform what they have come to personally experience, that in truth, is collectively part of us all to actualize. You may recognize in these people the aspects of Self as commonly identified archetypes, but notice how the individuals have come to experience them through their own life circumstances. What begins as a very personal journey for them, through this process, becomes an impersonal knowledge made conscious, of what lies deeply within our entire psyche to reconcile. Our bodies have given us an amazing vehicle in which to experience our individuality and experience our Soul. To reconnect with our true Essence, our Soul, is to liberate the impoverishment and suffering we have become attached to as our experience, and bring us to experience our Soul's presence in the moment. These case studies are not following a script to journey within, as many of these served to create structure for the Process of Inner Alchemy, as I have come to record it. Each session is as unique, as the patients were different, in how they could comfortably relate to what their body was expressing. When I do a session with someone, I go with him or her on his or her journey. I follow their energy, and am unattached to their experience, as I am the observer to help bring their awareness to the experience of the perception, that they have been separated from actualizing. I am not a guide in the process, as their energy is the guide, and it will always lead to source, if it is listened to carefully, and followed with faith, to where it is leading. I help people learn to focus on the subtle energy of the body, as it expresses itself through the layers of their experience. I feel their body energy, and for the time during the session I am them, in their thoughts, feelings and experience.

I haven't put names to these people, because it is not important *who* they are in this process, as much as what they have unveiled, about *what* they are. What we are is Soul. We are all beautiful beings with much to contribute to the experience of All. From embracing the journey within, through the Process of Inner Alchemy, we make gold from the fragments of raw Self that have become our experience of who we are, unrealized as being separate from Soul. Soul is perfect, so any other knowledge or perception we carry of our Self is not real to our true nature, and requires liberation to become one with us. There are absolutely no exceptions to this.

To work with children is much easier than adults in many instances because they can enter a process without wanting to have it all figured out ahead of time. I like to have a parent present, because there is a trust established there, that helps the child feel safe working with me. Also, the internal world of the child brings expanded awareness to the parents so they can better understand how better to relate to their child and meet their true needs. There is a magical transformation that takes place with everyone present at a session when a child reveals the internal Sensitivity. I am always in awe at what the body energy is able to reveal about a person, their perceptions and their unique road map to health. It is always a great honor to be witness to another finding their truth, especially when the parts of Self we have hidden away are many times common in their Essence to everyone of us in our own experience. As you read, you will have the opportunity to embrace how incredible the journey of transformation can be once entered with honesty. There is nothing anyone of us experiences that is beyond our ability to love and recognize in some form within us all. We are one in Essence, so healing an aspect of Self within, serves to move us collectively to heal the illusion of separation we have allowed to become our experience of who we are.

TEN-YEAR OLD BOY

Mother brought him in with the following information: Overweight, oversize for age, Pediatrician concerned that may have disease where growth hormones overactive.

When this boy came into my office his mother explained what the Pediatrician had told them and she was concerned that something else may be at the root of it. The boy's response to hearing his mother tell me about his health was to make jokes about himself and he avoided sitting down, making eye contact or willingly speaking with me.

Inner Alchemy Session:

He was nervously giggling when he first lay on the table, then he became very rigid and lay perfectly straight like a board with his eyes concentrated, closed.

I began the session by asking him to imagine he was breathing in through the top of his head and to just follow his breath down into his body as he exhaled. He was very still as if frozen.

I asked him what he felt. He replied 'Nothing'.

I asked him if there was a place in his body that the breath seemed to get stuck on its way down towards his toes.

He replied there was a spot on his right leg that felt pressure and was round and felt weird.

I asked him to really feel it and tell me about it. He jumped right into it because the next response he was already there.

He said that inside the bubble it was hollow and empty. It had very thin walls.

I asked if he could go into the middle of the bubble and tell me what was there.

He said there was nothing in there but him. Outside the walls of the bubble it was very noisy.

I asked him to step outside the bubble and tell me about the noise.

The noise he said was like traffic and then the traffic turned into a whole bunch of people around him. His body energy shifted significantly with this.

I asked how he felt in the middle of all those people.

He replied "happy."

His pulse was racing, and his body was visibly shaking.

I asked what his body was doing.

He replied, "it's shaking, but I don't know what that is"

I asked if this feeling was the feeling of happy to him.

He replied, "No."

I asked if he had felt this feeling before.

He replied, "Yes, but I don't know when."

I asked him if he would be all right to just be in the feeling of his body for a moment.

He was very uncomfortable and quiet but he was staying with the feelings.

He finally said the feeling reminded him of how he felt just before writing a test at school. It was exactly like that feeling. He named it as Nervous.

I asked him to go one more step and he would need to be brave. I asked him to let the nervous feeling get so big that he was in the middle of it. As he did his breath became shallow and his body wasn't shaking, it was more like frozen. I asked him to Name the feeling he had.

He said "fear." He stayed in it though and as he stood in the middle of the fear, it started to disappear. His body relaxed and tears started to roll down his cheeks.

I motioned for his mother to come closer to the table he was lying on, and she took his hand and just held it. She didn't say anything.

I asked him what was there when the fear disappeared.

He replied, "Me."

I asked how old he was there.

He told me, 'I'm 16."

I asked what 16 felt like.

He told me it felt very smart and helpful.

Then I asked him what 10 felt like.

There were tears and as he told me 10 was very sad.

I asked where 10 was? Was it inside or outside the bubble?

It was inside the bubble to him.

So I asked him to go inside the bubble to 10 again for a moment.

Standing in the bubble I asked him to tell me what the wall around him felt like.

He said the walls were melting and that he could walk right through them. He said they weren't really there anymore.

I asked if he felt he could be 10 and walk outside where he had been 16 before.

He said it was easy now.

Then I asked him to tell me how it felt stepping out there as 10.

His body energy was relaxed and his pulse was normal again. His energy was very expansive at this moment.

He said it felt "Good," "I am smart and I am helpful," then after a moments silence he added, "I'm good." He began to smile here.

I asked him if he thought he could be 10 now without being sad.

He said he could but that making mistakes made him feel bad so it was going to be very hard.

We talked about how mistakes are a way we learn. School is a place we go to learn, because if we knew everything we wouldn't need to go there.

He laughed because he thought it was funny that he was getting so upset with himself when he didn't know how to do things already. He said, at home though, it felt like he wouldn't be able do things right all the time.

His mom told him that it wasn't up to him to know how to do everything and that he needed to be able to talk to her when he was feeling this way.

He said he thought he could do that even though he didn't know what to do about it. He didn't like feeling like he wasn't smart enough to figure things out that were making him sad.

She told him that some things are for parents to help him figure out and he could help her understand how to do this better by sharing his feelings with her.

I asked him if he could tell me what the bubble was that he was in.

He told me it was his body being big with everything outside.

His mom and I both told him we thought that he was really smart and very helpful because we learned something very important from him that would help us understand him.

Following the Session:

He got off the treatment table and told me he felt really big which I thought was a great sign, in that his body has been expressing the illusion of big for some time now, yet within, in isolation, he had felt small and inadequate without even realizing it.

This boy's family situation is an ongoing challenge for him. His father has Multiple Sclerosis and his mother is the sole provider for the family. This boy is the eldest of two children and he had been growing at an accelerated rate since the age of 6. There were further sessions that followed this that went on to reveal his feelings about being responsible at home when his mother is not there. As he has become better at entering the energy of his body we have been able to go to the root cause of many of the decisions he had made at an early age in attempt to preserve his innocence and ability to experience it. He is now more aware of the food he chooses to eat and how he feels about himself in different situations. With each step he takes he is becoming more spontaneous and brings truthful humor to the sessions that is amazing for a boy his age. Identifying his emotions has been the biggest challenge for him. Most importantly as he learns to relate to his feelings he likes himself, and is learning that by expressing himself, those around him understand his needs better and are able to find ways to provide for them.

In this case I have used Inner Alchemy Therapy in conjunction with both Homeopathic Remedies and Nutritional support.

The blessing for me in this particular case has been the opportunity to work with each of the family members individually in context to their physical health. In their commitment to embrace their challenges individually, a synchronicity of the unseen dynamics within their family has revealed the great potential to move them all towards not only health of their physical bodies, but in healthy and fulfilling relationship to one another. As one reveals their Sensitivity, the others also benefit by understanding how best to facilitate nurturing and supporting of another's true needs. This family has demonstrated that Individualized Medicine can facilitate not only the true needs of an individual but because the emphasis is on the source of wisdom within, establishing integrity of Self within their life challenges remains aligned with healing, in its highest truth. The physical body bears witness by the resolution of the symptoms that represent the root cause of disease within them. To witness this family's courage in regaining health has been a great inspiration for me.

NINE-YEAR-OLD GIRL

Mother brought her in with the diagnosis of Juvenile Rheumatoid Arthritis and a history of Eczema

This child had been very sensitive to her environment and her mother told me her daughter worried about everything. She had repeated high fevers that spiked and then resolved without any other symptoms being expressed. There had never been any explanation for them. She had been home schooled because being in a regular school environment had created great stress and anxiety for her and she had experienced stomachaches regularly. She had been treated with Homeopathic Remedies since infancy and the mother had felt they had helped her daughter with various acute illnesses, but the eczema had persisted and now she had been diagnosed the Juvenile Rheumatoid Arthritis and the specialists were unable to control it or treat if effectively. The daughter was in a great deal of physical pain, and craved sweet food.

From the first time that I met this young lady I was completely captivated by her spark and incredible ability to articulate herself both emotionally and intellectually. She was bright, very clear in her expressions and talked easily with me about how she perceived things. She was a very optimistic young lady. The first time she came to my office she was with her younger brother and mother. Her knees were very swollen and she had made the trip with the help of a wheel chair because walking any distance was very painful. She had been taking Naproxen for a few months previous to her visit to see me as her arthritis was advancing quickly. I worked Intuitively with her from the first appointment, even though she also required aggressive treatment using Homeopathic Remedies and Nutritional support. Through my energetic testing using Auricular Medicine I found toxicity at the cellular level and an active virus in her system. Her Spirit though was magnificent. Her body needed help to get rid of the toxic overload and when I assessed her I found that she held many emotions, many of which were not hers. I knew she had much to show me about her ability to heal from this state of disease. She impressed me so much with her courage and willingness to express herself that my own intuition told me that to identify the underlying process that was functioning separate from her conscious state of awareness was going to be the ticket to turning this around quickly for her. Her mother was a Reiki practitioner so working with her daughter energetically presented no challenges in acceptance and support from home that she would have on her journey to health.

This particular case was not a defined Inner Alchemy Session with a beginning and ending. This young girl intuitively could express herself very easily when I would bring her attention to a specific energy the body was expressing. I was able to work with her to track it to where it was coming from as she became aware of it. I was assessing her with Auricular Medicine and finding remedies to facilitate her physical body to begin healing itself. As I would assess and treat an area, there was a pronounced energetic charge that would surface and she could feel the initial resistance and then shifts in her body. It became a matter of bringing her conscious awareness to her physical body and integrating what her Spirit was doing without her awareness, to heal herself instead of her processing energetically for everyone around her.

During the first appointment she identified her feelings of defeat by her illness. She told me she worried about her mother a great deal. When I asked her to tell me what it felt like when she worried about her mother, she went right back to the moment she remembered feeling torn between time spent with her father and her mother. She thought she could bring them together by not creating any problems. She didn't understand what was happening between them and as much as she loved her dad she was feeling really upset around him. There was much that the parents had been through together and her father had a serious addiction that she hadn't been told about. The mother began validating what her daughter was sensing by being truthful in acknowledging the problems the father was having.

Five weeks after her treatment with me, and taking remedies, the swelling and pain in her knees was gone, and she was walking normally. The Naproxen had been discontinued during that first five weeks, and within six months the Orthopedic Specialist had given a complete clean bill of health. The traces of toxicity on an energetic level were still there and would take some time for her to resolve, but physically she was in a state of ease again, and the Specialist could find no sign of physical imbalance within her system. It turns out that this young lady was very gifted intuitively and what she was sensing wasn't validated in what she was being told. Over the next year she worked with me to take the overload off her body so it could heal itself, and we also worked at finding ways to take the overload off her nervous system. She was integrating her natural intuitive abilities into her concrete world. In other words, she learned to trust her feelings and is now in school and involved with children and people outside her home. She is grounded.

She had felt that she couldn't move forward expressing her internal world without creating uproar in her home environment and creating more conflict between her parents. Her mom is a very aware and caring parent and had tried to protect her from knowing some of what she and her husband were dealing with. Since I started treating this young girl, her parents have divorced and her mom is remarried. She feels safe now and able to express her intuition brilliantly. She has many friends at school and is involved in many community activities now.

Worrying is what seemed to be the expression for her isolated Sensitivity. She worried about her mother, she worried about her father, she worried about their dog, her brother, other children, just about everyone that she was exposed to from a very early age.

When I asked her how it made her feel to worry about someone else she told me she became very tired. So we talked about the energy of worrying and she looked with her imagination at what sort of thoughts went with worrying. She discovered they were thoughts about being unable to do anything to solve problems others had to face, and how they looked too great to overcome. It was impossible to do anything she wanted to without leaving them behind to solve their problems on their own. When she described this to me I realized they were not the thoughts she had to face, but it was as if she were them, standing in their shoes. This was at the root of her physical symptoms. She wasn't expressing others symptoms, she had developed her own unique expression of the part of her Self being contained, as a result of the impressions she taking on of herself in these situation. She was resonating with them emotionally and mentally in hopes of easing their pain because she loved them. For her to fully embrace her own Sensitivity in the form of Intuitive Sensing she needed validation to know what she perceived was accurate. The underlying virus and dysbiosis that her body was challenged with went undetected because her nervous system was in the state of overwhelm.

She did really well recognizing when she had taken on another's energy and all was running smoothly until I received an email from her mother telling me that both she and her daughter were having a problem taking their vitamins all of a sudden. She told me her daughter was getting an upset stomach and couldn't bring herself to take them anymore and had asked if I could do anything about it.

After receiving the email that something had shifted, I called to speak with her.

I asked what was going on with her. She told me there was a court dispute between her parents over the father meeting the needs of his children, and she was feeling for him. Until that, she had been doing great. She sounded optimistic on the telephone but her body energy told another story. I told her I would check intuitively and see what was going on. The following is what came to me in response to the upset stomach and resistance to taking Vitamins. It was not what she was expecting but it worked to get them both on track with what supported health for them.

Worrier Becomes Spiritual Warrior

Worrying is draining and upsetting. When you are worrying about something that has to do with someone else, here is something to consider. For every moment we spend thinking about them, worrying, your energy is going to them- and it feels very draining because you are resonating with the negative funk they have got themselves into. Its like you are allowing yourself to 'feel for them' in the place they are stuck. They feel relief because

*you are taking on their problems- they feel no need to change anything.
How about trying this...
If we love someone, we think of all the things they do and mean to us that is good, kind and loving. That gets sent to them instead of all the worry. In sending this HIGH frequency vibration from us, we may have the effect of actually helping them to see things in a better light. We are letting them know we love them and that we would like relationship with them that is in the light and full of love. Both people benefit. This seems it would take the most work- remembering the good stuff people are capable of when they hurt us is hard- but when we send it our heart feels really great! Before you know it that person feels better too and they have been given a reminder to become the person you believed in all along. They get a reminder of their own high frequency.
So, I am sending to you tonight a reminder, especially for you. It's a memory of you when you came to Toronto and you, your mom and brother were having an adventure. You felt really great and your smile was brilliant. You walked with a skip in your step and you were thinking about all the things that were changing in your life that were making you feel very free and healthy. You are a very special person, and I love to see you when you are in your brilliance. This is the girl that has a lot of power to change and help those around her, by being YOU- this is the girl I believe in! I send this with a big hug because I am not the least bit worried about you! I know you can rise above those that get stuck- show them how- in this you are the expert! (more like genius actually)*

*love
Alison*

She is a healthy, vital and energetic fourteen-year-old now. She is doing great at school, is socially involved and has a wonderful outlook on life. Her mother's health on the other hand is now expressing the same symptoms that had been demonstrated by her daughter. In Chinese Medicine it is said that when a child appears sick- treat the mother. It makes perfect sense when we consider the impressions left within us about our ability to meet challenge, come from the impressions we take on of ourselves before we are separate form those we love. Through the unspoken and unrecognized knowledge they give us about what they believe they are, we believe we are the same.

The gift for me working with people intuitively is not just about seeing their health improve, but it is in the relationship they develop in trusting themselves and in turn trusting relationship with another. I have never found anything but pure goodness and light in anyone that has taken the journey within to embrace his or her Sensitivity. It is a joy to be part of another's journey to discover their personal power in healing themselves. The actual Remedies and Natural Medicine facilitate the body's natural ability to discharge what it has accumulated in the form of toxicity. The vitamins provide the nourishment that our foods and environment are unable to provide consistently anymore. These elements are just part of the support for what is ultimately an internal process and endorsement for their relationship with their state of EASE through the development of the positive aspects of True Self.

45-YEAR-OLD WOMAN

This woman had begun consciously working with her Intuitive gift of channeling Spirit in regards to people's health issues.

She currently works in the health field as an Occupational Therapy Assistant and Physiotherapist Assistant. She began to have congestion and a cough that was persistent, her blood pressure went up and she had to take some time off work.

This session revealed her Essence as the Goddess within. There in the middle of an Inner Alchemy Session she entered the sensation of being strangled. We tracked the sensations back to its origin when she decided it wasn't safe to express herself the way she chose. After neutralizing the emotion she was able to identify her fear as being in her own power, by being in it. As she lay there I heard the Goddess within her speaking to us. It was the aspect working with the higher truth of her Soul. I really wondered where this was going when her Goddess emerged with the mail, but I just relayed the message as it was being given to me and it led straight to her magnificence... and what a gift she is.

I didn't record the session so later that day I wrote it as I could remember it.... and to be honest, I think the Goddess within her was more poetic at the time of delivery.

Mail Reminds the Goddess

Along our journey it becomes inevitable that we are going to touch the Essence of our being within. It is terrifying to embrace such an incredible source of potential. It is there in each of us but we can have a difficult time wanting to hold it and align ourselves with it. It is camouflaged in fear. It is very scary to imagine what might be asked of us to embrace such a thing. The thought is overwhelming. To find inside that we are that special conjures up images of how heaven will deliver us into our magnificence from where we stand now. How is it possible for this little woman's body to conceal such power?

The fear would have us believing that in accepting our gifts, our true power, a huge crate that weighs ten tons is going to be dropped upon us from heaven and with its impact we will be crushed. This is our fear. This is a threatened ego, facing responsibility, painting a picture to deter us from a greater reality for ourselves.

Embracing our power in truth is more like collecting the mail from the mailbox each morning. Amidst a dozen envelopes of advertisements and bills, these being the illusions we have about who we are, is a letter personally addressed to us. Within this letter is a message that touches our Soul. It is from someone who loves us and recognizes the light within us. It is filled with optimism, support and gratitude for their relationship with us. We are joyful and elated to receive this message and having received it we are in turn filled with optimism about what that day holds for us. Naturally from us comes a joyful response to each situation and person we meet that day. That one letter is delivered to us in a form we can embrace, receive and integrate into our experience of ourselves that day. It comes under the guise of something that seems reasonable to us. We step into our power without even recognizing it - as it is a natural response.

Expressing who we are becomes a natural extension of the joy we feel inside at being recognized as special. Before we know it, opportunities present themselves to us to be who we are. We recognize them because it is a natural expression from us to respond to them. There is a gentleness and grace in accepting empowerment a bit each day. Even the bills seem manageable from this perspective.

The other envelopes in the mail, are the limited thoughts, ideas and actions that have served to clutter the way from us seeing our truth. With each reminder of who we really are arrive a handful of these accumulations in the same handful. Just like the bills, put these reminders in perspective, sort through them, and don't be afraid to throw out the ones that are junk mail. There is nothing to hold onto or analyze if it doesn't resonate with what you experience to be true. A bill is a bill, have a good look at it, give it acknowledgement and pay it respect so it may be filed in context and not clutter your desktop. It doesn't have power over you unless you invest your energy with it for the day by attempting to keep it at bay. Just take care of them as they come in.

The fear we feel in embracing our own power is a big puff of air. If we align ourselves with it, then those morning bills take on large proportions. The world seems bigger than us and our place in it seems hopeless. That one special message gets lost in the shuffle. If we allow ourselves to step right into the middle of our fear and really feel it, its truth is revealed as a big illusion and it disappears.

Invest in yourself because if the reminder of our potential is not delivered by post it will certainly be given in another ordinary way. It will make your day! Heaven on Earth is the message delivered and received in every day if we are open to receive it. Ten-ton crates do not drop from heaven, Just as we discovered the sky is not going to fall. Common sense gets lost when we allow ourselves to be diverted by fear. It is time to step into the light to reveal what has always been here, without fear. Our fullness and light in the name of Love And it is meant to be shared.

At the end of this message it all seemed a little more manageable to receive one's guidance and experience of empowerment in small increments of the ordinary experience of each day. This is a great message for us all to ease the fear of moving forward when we touch our magnificence with expanded awareness.

44-YEAR-OLD MAN

This man came in with no particular physical complaints that he shared with me, or anything specific that was wrong, except that he wasn't feeling genuinely happy in his life.

A very unassuming and sincere person entered my office and he had no idea what to expect with an Inner Alchemy session. He shared with me that having experienced success in his family life and career he had the luxury of taking some time away from his work to re-evaluate what would bring more meaning to him in his life. Coming to see me was on the recommendation of my husband who had treated him for some minor digestive complaints. There was nothing on the physical level that was posing any problems and yet he just didn't feel vital and happy getting up every morning. I told him as long as he was prepared to be honest with himself through the process, that there was nothing else he needed to know as the process itself would reveal to him what this was about, and that all we had to do was to follow the energy. I would help him to recognize the energy as it was revealed through his body.

Inner Alchemy Session:

He lay on the table and I sat behind him with my hands resting on his shoulders. I asked him to close his eyes and imagine he was breathing in through the top of his head and as he exhaled to follow his breath as it descended down through his body.

I then asked if there was a place that felt like his breath got stuck on the way down.

He didn't respond but his body became very nervous and fearful. It was as if he was frozen in that moment.

He was immediately in the energy of his body and didn't recognize it except in context to lying on the table.

It was here that I realized he had already developed the skills to be connected to the energy but no way of articulating or building relationship with it. In the middle of the energy he was frozen, so I guided him to rise up above and see himself as a tiny dot down below on the table.

His words came back once he was able to separate from the sensation that had taken over for him.

I asked him to trust his subconscious mind to take him back to the origin of this feeling so we could release the negative charge and be able to see it in clarity. He agreed.

So he surrendered to being taken back as if floating through the clouds until he felt like he had been stopped. I asked him to look down and imagine a line that represented every event that he had experienced from the beginning of time. Could he see a dot down below?

He shuffled his body in discomfort and said, "I don't think I'm doing this right. I can't visualize anything. I feel it but I can't visualize."

I asked him to remember the house he grew up in. Could he do that?

He said that was no problem.

I asked him if there was an image in his mind's eye when I asked him to remember that house.

Case Studies

He said, "Yes!"

I then explained that this is the same way that images of the unknown are shown to us. It is like a dream or movie clip in your mind's eye.

He relaxed because now he realized he could visualize very well.

He could see the line very clearly after all. I then asked him to go down onto the line he saw below him and tell me what it felt like to be the person he was there.

He did, and as he did this I realized he was standing beside another person down there. He had successfully 'side stepped' becoming himself at that time. His body energy was completely unchanged.

It was at this point that I realized this man was exceptionally aware of sensation and had been intuitively very engaged in his life without realizing what was being revealed to him because he had not developed a relationship with trusting his intuition.

I asked him who was standing in front of him.

As soon as I asked him this, his body energy shifted to be very anxious and hurt.

He immediately identified his teacher standing before him.

He had become a young boy and was now in that moment. He was experiencing the situation as he had at that time. That moment from the past had become in the now for him as he lay on the table and it was very uncomfortable.

He remembered it all very clearly and his body became very expressive now that he was the young boy again. I asked him to be with the sensations and allow his experience to be revealed through how he felt.

I asked him to just remain as the young boy for a moment so we could understand what the body was feeling and what he thought about himself or his life in that experience.

He was upset and feeling like he had no value. The teacher had humiliated him and made him feel worthless. He decided in that moment that he was worthless and would never amount to anything. He could do no right.

After identifying the truth of the young boy, I asked him to go up really high again into the heavens above. To leave the boy and see him as a tiny dot down below him. He had a bit of trouble with this as the emotional energy was very strong and to separate was difficult.

I asked him again to just be up above and look down and see the boy far away so he can't be recognized in detail anymore, just a dot in the distance.

Up high, once again I asked him to trust his subconscious mind to take him back before any of the events that led up to that experience. I explained we would come back to this place so he didn't need to worry about leaving that boy in that state of upset.

It took a few moments to be led back to before any of the events that led up to that experience.

His body relaxed and became very expansive when he reached that place.

I asked him to describe how he felt.

He said he felt calm and good; it was a feeling of nothingness.

I explained that here it is easier to ask that the negative emotions and sensations be released so that the polarity of the experience can be brought to consciousness. The mind had taken in everything in that situation, but only certain aspects of the situation were perceived because the emotional energy was so strong it served to separate him from the whole experience.

He visualized the negative energy leaving his body and then he visualized the positive energy coming in.

I suggested that there was no further purpose to holding on to the negative energy as it has served to bring him back to the place that there was something he needed now to reclaim in awareness in order to move forward with his life.

Once he had finished with the visualization of bringing in the positive polarity of his experience I asked him to return to the young boy. He didn't articulate what the positive polarity was, just that his body felt very full and weightless.

At first he didn't recognize being the young boy again because the emotional energy wasn't part of the experience of the boy anymore. But when he looked up as the young boy his teacher was standing there before him, so he knew it was him but he felt detached emotionally from the experience as if it was someone else. He saw this teacher in clarity now and his comment was that he felt a little sorry for this man that he had to treat him so badly because of his own feelings of inadequacy in knowing how to relate to him.

He said the young boy didn't feel badly anymore and knew that the teacher was not able to make him feel inadequate or worthless about himself. He knew he was a good kid who knew a lot, maybe just not the things that teacher could recognize in him. He honestly felt he hadn't done anything wrong and up until that moment hadn't realized what belief he had adopted from that situation.

Now that there was resolution and a greater truth had been realized,

I asked him to float up above the situation again. As he came back to the present moment, all the events and circumstances that had been experienced since that initial event with the teacher, that had a frequency or resonance with that experience would be healed. He could imagine that all the negative charges would be released and in their place the positive polarity would be actualized as part of him. All he had to do was place the intent that this would happen and the rest the mind would take care of for him.

I asked him to come back to the present on the table in my office and breathe in through the top of his head and down through his body again.

I asked how he felt?

He said he felt like an incredible weight had been lifted. He felt clear and good about himself.

I asked him to breath down into his body and get a sense of anything that might be needed inside himself.

He felt peace and gratitude within. He didn't feel he needed anything. He was feeling a bit disoriented, as he hadn't had time to assimilate all that had shifted within.

Following the Session:

He sat up and we talked about how this realization was significant to how he was currently experiencing himself in his life. He was still processing all that had happened and wondered how we got to this one incident?

From his energy sitting there, I read that he had been operating from the belief that everyone knew more than he did for a very long time without knowing it. He knew about things a different way, and possibly his teacher, and others in positions of authority hadn't always known how to encourage or endorse his expressions or Sensitivities.

He laughed because he wondered how I could know that. I told him it was right there in his energy to read.

I asked if he experienced this as true for him or could he relate to it? He could relate to this very well. He shared with me how he had become very successful in business but was very unconventional in how he approached and knew what decisions to make. As long as he worked alone there was no problem, but when it came to justifying to others his concepts he felt inadequate.

He told me about the people who had been approaching him to work with him and how amazing and knowledgeable and successful they were. He said he had been offered one specific partnership and was at a loss how to respond because he didn't understand how this person felt he would be a worthy partner. He honestly believed that they were more experienced than he was and yet they had been very insistent that he consider working with them.

I asked him if it was possible that this new partner had appeared to him just as the teacher had when he was a boy. Did he have the same feeling in his gut when the offer had been presented to him? He now recognized the origin of the sensations he had been experiencing with his digestion.

He sat there and was looking at this situation as if for the first time. He had been triggered by the opportunities being offered to him in regards to his work. Without being aware of it, his body had been expressing through sensation the part of himself that needed to be realized in order to recognize the call to step forward. To create relationship with that experience as a boy he had in Essence retrieved a positive perception of this particular aspect of Self that was now needed for him to experience Wholeness in the present.

Not until he reached the present time in his life and had the opportunity to grow in his work situation had this posed a limitation. He had learned to work alone and maintain his comfort zone for many years, but to move forward with a greater contribution he would need to change his mind about himself, specifically in regards to his worth, and in turn he would need to realize that he had become himself regarded by others as having authority in his field by his accomplishments. He was unable see this aspect in himself and until he realized his potential within that role to bring forth his uniqueness his digestive sensations would continue to get his attention. He had a negative experience of authority as a child, but now within him was the conscious knowledge of how to become himself a positive expression of authority greater than the one he had come to experience in youth.

    The interesting part of this Inner Alchemy session was the experience of the young boy with his teacher had instilled a hidden belief that others knew more than he did and that people in positions of authority were to be avoided because they made him feel worthless. He had been operating from this for some time in relationship to his work. He had experienced success with his career but he had limited himself to working alone. He already had experienced success in his unique approach to problem solving so he knew his abilities in this context. Now in his life there was potential and opportunities being presented, to work in partnership with others who had approached him as figures of authority and knowledge. He had never been able to realize this before because in similar situations he had in Essence become the young boy in front of the teacher and frozen in his tracks to know his value. All of his personal work in analyzing why he was not feeling happy deep inside kept him in his isolation from his Sensitivity that could further empower him in his life. To say that this is all that his search for fulfillment was about would be misleading, but in realizing this one gift he was free to step forward with confidence to a fuller experience of himself in context to his career, one that would be fulfilling and expose his skills to a wider audience to experience. I say this is the interesting part of the session because as we delve into the subconscious mind, and bring awareness to the underlying perceptions we have adopted, there is a commonality that influences us all. We all have our unique experiences that demonstrate these unconscious beliefs, but many of us share deep within our being, without even knowing it, the belief we are not worthy to be loved as we are. In our sensitivities, we feel exposed to criticism and being hurt, instead of empowered to illuminate the misconceptions that we encounter, so we may find understanding.

SEEING THINGS FOR WHAT THEY ARE...

Learning to follow the energy of our body takes practice, and learning to bring context to what is revealed in its truth, and our current experience involves integrating the various skills our mind is capable of. Often following a session, people are a bit disoriented, because not only have they come to unveil a truth within, but also with the one shift in perception there is a domino effect that although immediate on the energetic level, takes time to assimilate through their consciousness. Physical pain can be completely resolved within seconds of liberating the isolated aspect of Self in its truth. They will become aware of things that up until the session they were oblivious to even though it was right in front of them. They were unknowingly filtering it out, because of a limited belief held in isolation, from their awareness. One of my patients, a young woman in her thirties with Rheumatoid Arthritis, had a beautiful analogy to share with me on returning to my office one month after having had her first Inner Alchemy Session with me. I asked how she was and how she had felt over the last month. She reported that physically she was feeling overall better. Many physical symptoms had disappeared, and mentally she had experienced some ups and downs, but nothing unmanageable. Her experience following her session with me hadn't been anything like what she had expected.

Her words in describing her experience of her life since that session; "It is as if when I first walked into your office standing in my life was like standing on a very dusty floor. The dust had accumulated over such a long period of time that I never noticed it, even though I walked on it everyday. Then you came along and blew across the floor and all the dust was blown off the floor and into the air. All that dust became at eye level. All month I have been looking at the dust and seeing so many particles of what I have created as my experience over time. I can't believe it! I had no idea all that dust existed. And to have it at eye level has been very revealing. I have found the whole experience fascinating. I'm buying organic food and noticing all the healthy things out there, and meeting really nice people who are sharing information about things I never knew about before. So even though the dust is around me, I'm seeing through it and it's slowly clearing away." The part of her story that her words alone couldn't convey, was told through her bright eyes, dancing with the light in the room, as she spoke to me.

HEALING THROUGH THE PROCESS OF INNER ALCHEMY

A desire to heal is where it all begins with the Process of Inner Alchemy. It begins with the desire to transform a current negative experience, whether it's an illness, a perception, an emotion or a belief, into a positive experience. When we perceive something external to us as a threat then we are not in our Center. It is in the moment of acknowledging the negativity as our perception that we are reminded to take personal responsibility for our part in it. Not personal responsibility for the situation, or another in the situation, but of our perception of the situation. We cannot change our state of health, the environment, another person, or the world, without first changing ourselves. To continue thinking and doing things exactly the same way as we are currently, is not going to give us different results. So if we perceive ourselves in a particular way, this will not change unless we are able to heal that which holds this perception in place for us. If all our perceptions are great, and they make us feel authentically great, and we live in awareness of the positive potential in all our life circumstance, then there is obviously nothing to heal. We each choose what serves us and what doesn't and we make decisions consciously, or unconsciously, everyday based on what we choose to be our experience. We can discipline ourselves into taking different action, changing habits, and affirming positive thoughts but it is very difficult to 'will our way' in every aspect of our experience effectively and consistently based on external criteria for how we choose to be.

To go to the root cause of our actions, habits, thoughts, is to change the perception at the place of origin. Just like a domino, everything that has been built on that original perception, every compensation and adaptation we have made from our Natural State of EASE, knowingly and unknowingly becomes in line with our Soul. To change our Selves at this fundamental level means that the change is with us, part of us, integrated with who we really are, so we respond naturally from it rather than 'willing' the change to our conscious response in every circumstance. Identifying and taking care of our true needs is our personal responsibility. By taking the current perception and tracking it to its source within us we are liberating it into something that empowers us rather than continuing to further impoverish us. It is our Soul that carries such a map for our individualization.

It is Spirit, fueled by emotion, and revealed through imagination, that guides us back to our Soul. To become childlike, in our ability to look at something as if for the first time, full of wonderment and joy, is to be engaged with Spirit, in line with our true Source of knowingness. It is learning to hear our Soul with our heart that enables us to embrace and integrate a greater truth, and it is Spirit that carries us there on the wings of imagination.

Imagination is a wonderful word to describe what we call on because consciously unveiling the truth of the Soul feels too good to be true. It feels like something we would have to make up in our minds eye! In our Personal Power, in our Center connected to Soul, we know that we have everything we need at any given moment to carry out our purpose. All we have to be is open to receive, because Spirit will guide us to what we need to bring into our awareness that which best serves the situation.

PART FIVE:

Finding Our Way Back to the Origin

BEING IN OUR CENTRE

*T*o be in our center is to be aligned with our greatest truth that we are aware of within us. To be in our center is to consciously align and connect with our divinity within, our Soul, through the perceptions of awareness. In our center we know that we have choice and resources within us to perceive with clarity that which the current experience is offering us in its truth. To be in our center we are able to discern what is being shown to us in all its truth, not just the way we perceive through our own experience. To align with the Source within, we are guided in a current experience, to what will reveal the potential present, to be who we are in a fuller expression. Being in our center is to acknowledge that we place faith in something greater than ourselves and surrender ourselves to the process of unveiling a greater understanding. We come to see our part clearly and step forward with our contribution having faith in our inner guidance to have the gift in the moment be revealed to us through the process.

For those of us that have not yet come to know God within, in some aspect of our being, it is to come from our heart, to be honest and direct with what we speak and believe to be the truth at that moment because the external poses no threat to us. It is to relinquish the idea that in exposing our weakness and Sensitivity we will be placed in danger. In our center we feel bigger than our challenges, and draw on courage and strength from our internal resources. In being in our center we acknowledge that we can change our minds, be inspired by others to realize a greater reality for ourselves because we are open to receive what others bring forth into our awareness that can elevate us to a fuller understanding of ourselves and in turn see them in their light. We can come closer to knowing our Soul through the process of trusting ourselves and through the act of being openly honest with others. To know God in the many expressions is to know our Self in our many expressions. Different aspects of Self can come to be one with God at different times, through the process of integration. Being open with where we are at in the moment, and allowing others the opportunity to mirror our limitations to us, in hopes of liberating them into a truer expression of our Soul.

Coming back to our center, when triggered, requires acknowledging and accepting the aspect of our Self that is engaged so we may be realigned with a greater expression of who we are. We relinquish our expectations in the outcome of current circumstances and allow ourselves to be guided by the energy presented instead of relying on the limited expression that words provide. By remembering to engage the components that make up our awareness at the conscious level it means we have empowered our Sensitivity, to embrace the gift that it serves to develop in us. We successfully dissolve the wall of illusion that holds our Sensitivity separate, when we accept our feelings in the moment, and allow others to experience us in our present truth. By becoming present in awareness we are engaging in the possibilities that Spirit can bring into our experience. All aspects of mind eventually become in harmony and in line with what we choose to come forth with from the level of our Soul. Our actions become natural and authentic expressions of who we really are, perfect in their ability to enable us the experience of growth.

To be in our center in some arenas in our life is going to be easier than others. There are many aspects of our humanness that bring forth different expressions and aspects of us. It is through the act of learning to trust our inner guidance that we can come to realize many of them in their full and positive expression. Our intuitive abilities take us past our limited perceptions to the origin of their inception so we can create harmony between who we are presently and what we choose to be in line with our potential. As we resolve the various aspects of ourselves, the archetypes, we have come to identify with such as the mother, the healer, the warrior, the rescuer, and the many other expressions we have come to experience, we become Selfless. Our awareness takes us beyond these limited perceptions of positive and negative, light and shadow aspects of Self, to come from the level of what we really are, our Soul, where the polarities are perceived symbolically. Whether we experience the polarities of each of these aspects is irrelevant once we have become connected with our Soul as we see them as balanced and in harmony with a fuller expression of what we are.

Many of us are able to be in our center professionally as the aspect of Self that brings a certain expertise to the forefront, but on the home front we fail to hold center when challenged with the routine of everyday life with family. If we could all take the time to recognize and care for our true needs at exactly the moment we need to, than it would be a lot easier to maintain our center. Life has a way of getting hectic, and demands of colleagues, spouses, work, children, friends and family can be difficult to juggle if we overextend ourselves attempting to meet other's expectations of us. These expectations are based on our programmed beliefs about what a good mother or father is. What a good spouse is. What a good friend is. What it is to be good in our chosen field of expertise. Before we know it, we are feeling out of control, and doubting ourselves, and it is hard to pinpoint what can change without further plummeting into the experience of failing to meet our responsibilities to others, and the expectations we perceive they have of us. The minute we doubt ourselves we are not coming from our center. We have engaged all that is not in harmony within us, and our perception of our external world reflects it back to us. Who's expectations are we really failing to recognize anyway?

Bringing it back to Self reveals the truth of what assumptions we sometimes place on others perceptions unknowingly.

Being honest with ourselves about what we need on a deeper level is to become aligned with our True Self. Not what we would like, or what we don't want to happen, but what we need, honestly to feel at peace with it all. If we meet the needs of our physical body, our intellectual body, and our emotional and spiritual body are we not in a better position to recognize how to better serve another? Being clear with our Self, in honesty, maintains holding our center and it brings awareness on the subtle levels of our own experience through honoring our integrity and sincerity of words and actions with others. Beginning an honest dialogue within helps us to recognize what we are operating from, and whether we are being true to our Self and what we need to be in harmony with our Self. As soon as we doubt or question ourselves in relation to what other people think, we are not in our center. We have stepped out of alignment with our internal references and guidance that is true for us. We get into who we think is right, not what feels right within us. Much of the pressures we experience we come to realize as self-inflicted because we are trying to facilitate and be responsible for more than is physically, mentally or emotionally possible for us to control in others. We take on what is not ours to take on to begin with in the hopes of keeping our Self safe from embracing our real needs on the emotional/spiritual level. Our need to control everything around us becomes the compensation for us attempting to control all that is stirred within us that we wish to avoid because it is uncomfortable. The more we experience life void of Self awareness, the better we become at orchestrating events and relationships with others to keep us in our comfort zone. We subconsciously avoid placing ourselves in situations that will promote growth in an attempt to maintain our perception of security.

Infants, children, pets and those not capable of meeting their own needs require assistance, but it is perhaps better to facilitate them from our center so they can come to experience the best part of us, and in turn are inspired to reach for the best part of themselves. To care for another in need is a great joy when we come to experience them from our center, because we come to see and experience the part of them that is beyond their currently exposed limitations. It endorses placing faith in their abilities. It becomes a privilege for us to be part of their experience while they learn and experience their part in it, and feel free to express it, as it is emerging, knowing they are safe to be who they are with us. Those we care for in truth become our greatest teachers because of what they call forward to appear from within us to be actualized. Limitations that we perceive in others are ultimately our own as we have failed to place belief in something greater than us all, the Source of All where we are all magnificent in our individual expressions and as One.

HOLDING SACRED SPACE

To hold Sacred Space for another is to be in our center to receive them in whatever expression of who they are at that moment, keeping the image of them in our awareness, in their ultimate perfection, so they come to find clarity for themselves. To hold Sacred Space for another is to believe in another to find their own truth and be willing to hold space that is safe and supportive of their own internal process. To hold Sacred Space as I am defining it is not about creating an actual Sanctuary in terms of ritual and architecture, like a Temple, as we have come to know them. It is about energetically resonating with the innate goodness and strength in another that provides the opportunity for them to go beyond their currently held perception to realize the deeper belief or need that yearns to be recognized. Both an actual Sanctuary and Sacred Space are lined up with the same Divine Essence, but Sacred Space as I am referring to it here is about creating the experience of Sacred Space within the context of everyday experience. Our spiritual, mental and physical bodies become our personal Temple for our individual experience of Soul, as part of the All. Regardless of culture, belief, or origin of birth, our Temple, as Sacred Space is accessible to us in our own way. It requires allowing what appears to be the experience of distance with others, to emerge in its truth, on the conscious level, so our adopted compensations can be recognized, and our currently held perception can be liberated to dissolve the illusion of separation. To hold Sacred Space brings awareness to a conscious level, so our deeper needs and desires can be realized, without the adopted patterns that have served to give us a false sense of being satisfied. The illusion of the experience of separation is revealed by us and a greater truth acknowledged by us, not by another defining what they believe our experience represents to us.

For us to make a shift in our perceptions we have to change something inside ourselves, whether it is acknowledgement of a deeper need, or a sincere desire that has gone unrecognized. If another fails to hold Sacred Space for us, our illusions are further endorsed and we become further separated from our truth. It takes great courage to hold Sacred Space for another because we can be perceived as betraying them. The experience of having someone hold Sacred Space for us can be interpreted as being left behind, ignored or misunderstood. Holding Sacred Space is not jumping on another's bandwagon to help justify keeping their perceptions intact and their perception of an external villain supported. I am not suggesting that we decide for others what serves or doesn't serve them for this is for them to decide. But to bring them back to what and how they are honestly experiencing themselves in the present moment, brings integrity to their own inner guidance aligned with True Self. Many of us don't recognize the compensations and games we engage in to get our needs heard and met. We've been tricking ourselves for so long we aren't able recognize it anymore. It is not until we feel the distance between ourselves and others that we come to entertain the idea that something is not as it should be because we don't feel good.

We all have the ability to adopt very complex ways to engage others in our illusions. We become masters of orchestration to get our needs met, and we do it subconsciously most of the time. Our experience of separation is a perception we have that stands in our way of seeking a transformative truth. To liberate our perception most of us need to acknowledge that something has to change and when others fail to support us we initially try to figure out where they are coming from. It is not always another holding Sacred Space consciously for us. But a higher aspect of another, in Spirit, can hold Sacred Space even if they aren't conscious of it. Is our perception of their lack of support because they don't *agree* with us? Or is their lack of support their inability to *relate* to or endorse our current perception? What if we are in our light and it makes others uncomfortable to be around us because they are triggered to question themselves? How many of us use this reasoning to justify separation? It keeps us feeling justified, and definitely superior, but does it help us feel love for another in the situation? If we see the other through the eyes of love than maybe in our power we are making others uncomfortable, because they now face the opportunity to grow as well. In our power, we see others through the eyes of love and believe in their ability to meet their challenges as well. If we feel superior, then possibly we have some hidden belief that needs to be liberated to experience the joy in sharing and growing with another, knowing we all have something to learn in every situation. Diversity is the color and flavor of life. In any given situation, we can create the experience of separation from our True Self by trying to figure out what is going on with other people, and what they think of us, and do they know more than we do? We can get into a loop of Self-doubt and confusion if we begin placing our faith in what the external world shows and endorses in us. In order to come back to a state of balance we need to be able to find a reference for ourselves internally, so we can define what we need to be true to Self.

Our integrity, our truth is ours alone to perceive, and when we reach it in honesty, we find everyone else there as well in the light. To recognize this, is to embrace the truth that diversity is also the passion in life. In not recognizing when to hold Sacred Space for another we betray ourselves, in keeping ourselves separate from the experience of rejoicing in another's ability to unveil and experience their magnificence. One person in their light is a benefit to us all. We can receive such a blessing in the simple act of bringing awareness to holding Sacred Space for another.

To hold Sacred Space for another is to surrender to what the situation has to reveal in its truth. All we can do is listen to others with an open heart, and resonate with what lay under their current perceptions, to see a clearer Self in them through their body energy. To play back what others say to us, helps reveal the limitations of our current perception, and understanding we have of them in the situation. To hold Sacred Space is to be present with another, even when we disagree with them, and placing faith in speaking our truth with them. It is to be still, to be compassionate, to be open to hear what they express to us, and summoning the courage to honestly respond from our own heart. Even if all we know of them is that somewhere inside they are hurting, and that they too have God within to illuminate truth to them, in a way they can relate to, and accept to move them to a greater understanding of themselves and us. Holding Sacred Space is to facilitate the unveiling and expressing of their own truth, as it is revealed through their unique perceptions of their experience.

To hold Sacred Space can be a rendition of the 'tough love' approach. It sometimes requires stepping back and allowing another the opportunity to experience the consequences of their choices, while maintaining a safe environment for receiving them. For some this is how they come to understand themselves for they can't acknowledge their part in it any other way than through the physical act of experience.

To experience something is to come to know it on many levels, whether consciously or not. It may be that to step back and allow another their experience is to open the door of possibility to want to seek a better way. It is very difficult to help ourselves if we are under the illusion that we are the recipients of random action of others toward us and placed in unfortunate circumstances without choice as to how we respond to them. To acknowledge our own responsibility of our perception is to embrace the concept of seeking within answers that can satisfy us. We are further plummeted away from the experience of Wholeness if we cannot accept that the obstacles we perceive as external are ultimately derived from an internal source and we are personally responsible for maintaining them, or liberating them into a greater truth. All the excuses in the world will not change what is, they will just prolong the inevitable of facing our Self in its truth.

To hold Sacred Space for another is to believe in another's ability to find their own truth, and to graciously accept their perceptions without judgment or criticism, as they are unveiled in the layers that have come to separate them from the experience of Wholeness. The gift in holding Sacred Space for another is the faith entrusted to hold true to the belief in them, in their ability to return to Wholeness, in their power and grace of who they really are, not what they have shown us unconsciously in fear and weakness.

AWAKENING TO INNOCENCE

Through the Process of Inner Alchemy, in reclaiming the lost parts of Self, we return to the state of seeing our world through the innocent eyes of a child. To be reconnected to our Soul with faith in our intuitive abilities is to regain faith in Self, others, and the goodness that lies within us all. Innocence is the experience of love that is the perfect unique expression of our Soul. As adults it is what completely captivates us in embracing, and loving babies and children of both human and animal origin. They reach right past our illusions of the life experience and touch the part of us that knows this truth of pure goodness found in our Soul. In the experience of innocence we are also exposed to all that has the potential to misunderstand, wound, hurt or jeopardize our sense of safety.

To reclaim innocence is to reconnect with Soul, the part that is never tarnished in any way no matter what has been done to us or been experienced by us. There is much healing that lays between what Truths the Soul retains and what the various aspects of Self have come to experience as a segment of truth. Confusion can be a mechanism to keep us separate from an inner knowing that is aware of the truth of the Soul. What we consciously think, ego, can become engaged to protect what has been violated and we are unable to see it any other way because there is overwhelming emotion still in place for us. Confusion is a symptom of lack of integrity on a fundamental level of our Being because we hold the perception that our innocence has been violated somewhere along the line. The misperception of our confusion can serve to keep us aligned with our inadequacies and the inadequacies of others who violated our trust. Or we can relinquish our currently held perceptions of past events, to embrace the truth of our own innocence that must be acknowledged in order to find forgiveness and healing for our Self.

We can't change the event, or pretend that it is all right for someone to violate our trust, but we do have the power to transform our experience of it into something that strengthens us and supports growth and fulfillment for us. Forgiveness of those that violated our sense of safety to be who we are, can only be realized when we reclaim our own innocence in it, for it is in this act alone we are open to perceive another's innocence as well. That may seem like a big stretch, but when we acknowledge in ourselves Truth, as it exists, the forgiveness and clarity naturally follows. This is not a mental exercise by any means, because this level of truth goes beyond cognitive reasoning and can be obtained only through feeling with our being. Our Awareness has the ability to end the misunderstood expression of violation, as horrible as it can be, and liberate it into something that has created an opportunity to develop in strength a part of our Self that may otherwise have remained dormant. This in itself is a big leap of faith but we are all capable of it through allowing our intuition to guide us to the truth of our Soul.

GROUNDING

Like everything else I've come to know, the way I finally understood what it was to be grounded came in a very ordinary way. Building shelves brought me back into my body. I didn't know I was out of my body to begin with, so the experience of being grounded was a different sensation that felt odd at first but very calm. I have my husband Mikhael to thank for this home remedy. We were setting up our first office together, and there were shelves that needed to be assembled for the pharmacy. I had to get the shelf pieces out of the boxes, organize them and then follow the directions and hammer pegs in place to hold them together. I can't remember feeling more challenged in my life. I have an independent streak that luckily fueled me to figure it out for myself. After all, it was just assembly, not rocket science. I really had to concentrate at the task at hand. As I rolled up my sleeves and began the project I started to really enjoy doing it.

The rest of the world on all levels seemed to fade into the background. A few hours passed and it felt like I had been working on those shelves for only half an hour. I felt this full, calm feeling in my body and everything around me seemed very manageable. I didn't feel in a hurry to finish, and I was thoroughly enjoying the process of these shelves taking shape into a wall unit. I really liked the feeling that project had given me the opportunity to experience. I was grounded. I wondered if I had actually ever been grounded before because this feeling felt like I had just stepped onto solid ground after being at sea for the first part of my life. There was a stillness and clarity that accompanied this sensation.

What I realized was that I was grounded and my body felt heavy in a full way, not heavy in weight. Movement in my body was fluid and effortless and I was present with all aspects of the project. If there were an adequate way to describe what Wholeness feels like, it would be at that moment of realization that I felt close to it. It didn't feel like the thoughts in my head were running a separate dialogue from the task my body was engaged in. The whole experience of this process of building shelves seemed seamless and complete. It wasn't about building shelves at all; it was about focusing in the moment without distraction. My intellect was engaged, my physical body was engaged and my emotions were peaceful, all focused on the same thing and Spirit was One with me in the process.

Of course there are only so many shelves one can build in one's life so I took the components of the experience and started to bring awareness to being engaged in mind, body and Spirit with whatever I was doing at any given moment. Now the advice I received about getting grounded made perfect sense, and I am not sure why I hadn't been able to grasp what people were telling me, except that I didn't understand that it required focus on ground level activity.

My garden has since become my Sanctuary because it grounds me. I move stones around, pull weeds, plant vegetables and herbs and tend to my garden during the spring, summer, and fall. I love being in my garden. I can hardly wait to get out into my Sanctuary. It allows me to become present with nature and myself again without other people or their energy to distract me from my inner world. The physicality of the work brings my focus into what I am doing and I can hear Spirit more clearly when I have my hands in the earth and connected to what Earth reveals to me about herself.

Most of my inspirations come while working in my garden. Something magical happens when we are grounded. Nothing is "out there" to perceive in its illumination, it feels natural and part of us, complete in its understanding. I work with homeopathic remedies with my patients and being engaged with Nature has revealed to me the Spirit and Essence of the precious earth energies through the plants, minerals and animals. We have about twelve cats at any one time, and a few litters of kittens born each spring, that live outside around our house. There are rabbits that come around the vegetable garden at dusk when they think the coast is clear and nibble on wild lettuce that grows outside the gate, and sometimes we are blessed with a deer crossing our land on its way cross country. To be in my garden is to become the observer of these animals and the way they are in their natural environment. My garden is out back away from the house and close to the forest edge. It is easy to hear the trees and birds out there. It is very affirming to be in Nature as it reveals a natural way that it cares for itself and one another. We don't interfere with the cats in the way they handle their young, and when we have nature has found a way to right the wrong of interference.

I have rescued a few of the newborn kittens when the mother has left them under a bush or out back by the garden if they are sick or weak. She has placed them apart and tended to her healthy litter without another thought of leaving them. I've brought a couple of these kittens in the house to rub them into breathing again, feed and care for them, when they were exposed to the cold for too long. Whenever I have rescued one of these kittens, the mother has taken them back in, but later something else has happened to them. One was brutally attacked by some wild animal one night and killed. Others I thought I had "saved," later on met some other demise that left me feeling heartsick. The cats have taught me to let them take care of themselves in their own way. Nature can seem brutal when we witness it through our own perceptions, yet kind and just in its reverence to Nature's Power to balance herself in its truth.

In my mind, my garden was a private retreat for me, to step out of the world for a time, and enjoy the magic of nature and integrate whatever the day had brought me. That was my perception until an incident that happened very unexpectedly one day. I needed to understand that we step out of the world, as we perceive it, and enter it in an expanded awareness, which is inclusive of the polarities of our perceptions, when grounded. Retreat, separation, and solitude on the energetic level are an illusion, and finding peace requires being open to accept the parts of ourselves that are subconsciously guiding us towards experience that will illuminate where we have created separateness in our perceptions. Growth feels painful as long as we don't accept what it is guiding us to realize in our truth in the present. I have put in parenthesis through this story this experience as it relates to the Process of Inner Alchemy.

One day I went out to my garden with the illusion of stepping out of this world for a time to rejuvenate and reconnect with my Soul. I closed the gate and started into the jungle of onions this particular day. There was a mommy cat expecting her babies any day and she was following on my heels that day, complaining and rolling over in front of me whenever I stopped. As I began pulling the onions, there she was a foot away lying on her back, rolling in the weeds telling me her woes. Some of the other cats were playing in the plants and pouncing at bugs having a great time. They all seemed to fade into the background as I worked. Then I glimpsed something out of the corner of my eye move in the jungle of overgrown onions. I looked but didn't see anything. I heard a rustle this time and still couldn't see anything. So, I dismissed it and figured it was my imagination or the wind moving through the brush. So, on I dug, loosening the onion bulbs, reaching down and pulling up handfuls of onions and weeds to sort them out. This process became a meditation. Then something jumped out at me as I reached down to grab a bundle. To say I was startled is putting it mildly because I was beside myself for a moment. As I stood there I saw it was a very big, old toad, the size of my hand. (*I was triggered!*) He jumped on the wooden side of the garden box and just sat there. I went back to pick up my trowel and this incredible wave of grief went through me. I stopped in my tracks and looked back at the toad. There was blood dripping from his back leg where it had been severed, and he looked directly at me. *(I recognized an aspect of Self was engaged because of my reaction rather than a response as observer- it felt personal to me. I accepted my emotions as they came without analyzing them, just feeling them intensely, and was led through them to a deeper experience of truth within me)* In that moment, he was no longer a toad, I saw a soldier who had been wounded and he was dragging his leg trying to get out of the line of fire. I felt fear in this image, and then incredible guilt. *(It was really hard to be with this imagery because the emotion of it was intense and very uncomfortable. I just stayed with it to see what it would reveal that I could relate to.)*

In my carelessness, with my trowel in hand, I had been the line of fire for this old toad. My understanding of that garden changed that day. *(I took responsibility for experience and sought to accept my part in the incident)* It was my Sanctuary, and home to others. To think that I could leave the rest of the world outside its gates is to disregard the Sanctuary as a means of sustenance and safety for all of earth's life forms. *(I became observer of what symbolically was being shown to me in being present in the moment, and in being with it, it was no longer felt about me personally, but my expression of a collective perception)*

In being grounded, I acknowledged that my garden does not belong to any of us really, but sustains and cares for all that inhabit and respect honor it's system of balance. The toad was the great teacher that day, and reminded me of something very important. The world, in my attempts to consciously step out of it that day, was experienced in full color, full intensity, and through me, as I am of this earth. Being grounded reveals life magic, but often it is the polarity that first shows up, disguised as isolation, and limitation of our experience as humans, walking this earth. The pain I felt that day was mine as much as the toads, and I was very grateful that incident revealed my responsibility for my part in it. *(My personal manifestation of the collective perceptions took me a few days to understand because I was blind to the perception I was holding subconsciously.)* That open wound on that toad, unleashed so much grief, that I hadn't acknowledged before within me. Anger that was concealing my grief, was acting through me, without me even realizing it. In entering my garden as a Sanctuary, I was shown symbolically through my relationship with that toad, the limitation of my conscious perception of "stepping out of my day," without even realizing it was my attempt to step out of what I had subconsciously perceived as "being in the line of fire in my life experience." That toad broke the illusion of actually being able to avoid anything, by giving me the experience of becoming the line of fire within the safety of my Sanctuary. I became what I had unknowingly feared most- being hurt in the line of fire. *(Integrating the polarities of Self in full spectrum)*

My garden is a Sanctuary for healing through the act of grounding me. I hadn't seen it from that perspective before and had more compassion for what can appear to be the line of fire in its truth. Our fear, anger, and hurt, when not acknowledged still exist within us, and has the ability to in turn harm another without our realization. It acts through us without our awareness until it shows itself to us in what we experience. Earth in her receptiveness served to support me that day, by taking the fear and grief in its overwhelming state subconsciously within me, and transforming it into a greater awareness. An awareness that showed me the shadow of an aspect of myself, in all that I had previously seen as threatening in others, towards me in my life. It was me all along that was resonating with the same in others. That toad was an angel in disguise. And thank goodness he is alive and well today in my Sanctuary. *(the blessing offered in the incident)*

What happened in my garden that day was very helpful in articulating the Process of Inner Alchemy on a conscious level for me. I believe it is our natural ability to move towards clarity if we place the integrity back into our relationship with True Self. Inner Alchemy is a conscious journey that we become more proficient at, and can be used to move our Self past any current experience that doesn't feel good. It doesn't mean we will change the situation, but we can keep ourselves from developing further compensations in order to live with ourselves, by changing our perceptions. It doesn't matter how much Inner Alchemy I do, I am not ever going to believe that hurting the toad was all right to do. I made peace with the incident and accept responsibility for my actions. I am also grateful that the toad had jumped forward to play his part in it as well. Hopefully, in recognizing the fear and hurt in myself sooner I will not create such an expression of it again and that toad allowed me to heal a part of Self I had not realized that I had separated from.

Grounding, as an important component to the Process of Inner Alchemy, is to give the focused yang, masculine energies of Heaven, fueled by our desire to heal, a means to connect with the yin, receptive feminine energy of Earth. It is through our amazing physical bodies and our mind's ability to illuminate and integrate the polarities of a given perception, that we come to transform our experience into something that unites us, in our masculine and feminine qualities, with our Soul, one another and the ALL.

To be grounded, quite simply, is to allow our Spirit to be in our body.

IN THE REALM OF OUR GARBAGE

There is a place in the realm of heaven that I call Garbage Land. It seems that we all go through an initiation process of sorts when learning to work with our intuitive abilities. This layer is like the maze of all the different representations of energy on other planes of existence.

It is the world of our psyche and learning to navigate it demands doing a few loops and back flips trying to decipher which way is up. Our perceptions can become very much on the edge of losing touch with this physical reality. It is in Garbage Land we learn to walk the edge between Heaven and Earth with skills to navigate and perceive reality in its many dimensions and in its different levels of truth. Channeling of Spirit and what many have defined as Guides, Angels, and Entities, all requires becoming familiar with Garbage Land whether we want to or not. Garbage Land is what I call this chaotic level because it is where all the Spirit connected to human form enters our awareness, and it must be acknowledged, in order to gain clarity for ourselves.

In awareness we enter this realm, as it is the accumulated garbage of the intellect that we have failed to recognize in its freeform state. The garbage represents the parts of Self we have neatly compartmentalized so we can create a sense of order within, and when unleashed, appear to be a mess! I call it Garbage Land because to me initially it is all that we are resonating with unconsciously that is not true to Soul, and just as long forgotten landfill sights emerge as threats to our ecology, these dump sites of our psyche have become the source of our internal toxicity. All the parts of Self that seek resolution are out engaging with Spirit that resonates with a similar energy pattern, and we are functioning completely separately from any awareness of it. Our conscious mind, before entering garbage land, has been working completely separately from our Spirit, and our emotions are subconsciously fueling what experiences our Spirit is drawing to us, in hopes of making aware what is within contaminating our perceptions. It is not until we connect consciously with Spirit that we begin to experience all that we have inadvertently engaged with on the energy level.

We learn the importance of focus within, and our intent for Self in Garbage Land. By recognizing the chaos as the internal environment of unrecognized perceptions we have allowed to accumulate, through unconsciousness, we become empowered to embrace the clarity of Soul again. We also learn to trust our mind again through internal focus, because it is the only guide that can navigate such an immense amount of information and provide clarity as to what we can consciously assimilate, in relation to our personal experience. Garbage land is where we learn to observe our thoughts, what they resonate with, and how to become diligent in accepting responsibility for them. In unconscious focus, we evoke all kinds of energy that resonates with our separateness from truth. There is a Self-regulating system in effect in the world of energy. To abuse the privilege of intuitively engaging in another's perceptions is to bring further havoc to our own experience on many levels, if we are filtering them through our own limited perceptions. The further we get from truth within, the more chaotic and uncontrollable our external experience becomes. There is also forgiveness ever present with the realization of truth, because in the higher realms of consciousness, there is no good or bad. Forgiveness, unfortunately, doesn't mean we will not experience that which we initiate consciously or unconsciously. We continue to feel badly, as long as we are not open to change what ultimately is within us, in our limited beliefs of possible outcomes.

This is why I have come to work specifically in relation to the perceptions held in relation to the physical human body. It is quieter, and the body sensations specifically relate to the disease state of the individual's body. The information that is directly linked to the physical structure of an individual, whether it is present in actual symptoms, the emotional, spiritual or mental states, it all specifically relates directly to their personal perceptions of their experience. In attending to the physical body's energy as a beginning place, it becomes easier to build on what we currently can relate to as it exists, and unveil the origins of the states, as the individual has come to experience them.

Ultimately, we move more deeply within, past the individual experience, into collective beliefs. This becomes a natural process, through actual experience, rather than beginning by trying to fit into what others have defined for us through the intellect. The layers beyond garbage land are much smoother sailing but we have to become proficient and comfortable with our navigation skills to be able to cut through the chaos of the lower frequency energies that consume us. It requires being able to cultivate stillness within, bringing awareness to our thoughts, so we can establish focus to our body sensations and subtle energy. Learning to listen internally is being able to ground energy efficiently by becoming comfortable with being led in awareness by the energy within. For me this Garbage Land is what appeared to me first in my experience and it was some time before I learned what everyone was talking about when they would tell me " you have to get grounded." They gave me advice to eat red meat, to get outside and walk on the land, to lie on the ground, to work with the soil and to be in nature as much as possible. I did all of these except the red meat, because taking an iron supplement seemed better than feeling the fear of the animals in the meat. As I did all of these suggested things my mind was operating everywhere but in the moment, so my garbage was coming right along with me. There was no peace or shutting it off. It was like trying to work when someone keeps interrupting even though you've asked them to wait a moment. To stop and hear these thoughts rather than trying to "turn them off" hadn't occurred to me at that time.

Apparently I had a lot of myself operating without awareness, and I needed to clarify for myself what parts of me were engaging subconsciously. I had an incredible amount of learning and healing ahead of me and this was becoming more obvious. I honestly didn't understand what it meant to be grounded. I also hadn't realized that I could control what I was doing. How I didn't know that is beyond comprehension now, but at that time I honestly didn't feel I could do anything to change what was happening in my life or to me. Hopefully the way I have shared my understanding of what it is to be grounded will facilitate any of you who missed the boat along with me when it came to that remembering lesson. We all need reminding to be in the moment with our hearts present, not just our thoughts. It simplifies things considerably.

OUT OF CHAOS COMES POTENTIAL FOR CLARITY

To become clear we need to touch a reality that we understand in relationship to our current experience. How can we be in our center if we haven't been able to identify our own thoughts from the jumble of noise going on in our head? I wondered when I first became aware of all the information that was consciously in my awareness, if my experience was similar to a toddler learning language. Out of peoples mouths would come words, and from their Soul came different words. It was as if part of their mind was answering exactly what they were feeling even though consciously they would answer something different. I came to relate the information as coming from the Soul because it was sincere and there was no hiding their true feelings and perceptions about what they were being. I was trying to figure out what was going on. Then, I would meet someone who's Soul actually matched what they were saying out loud, or what they were doing. I have to tell you, these people in my experience have been very few and far between. I honestly don't think people are lying to one another on purpose- just disconnected to their truth, or afraid others won't honor them for their truth. We develop the skill of telling half truths, or benevolent lies, because we don't want to come short of another's expectations of us. This is a very interesting way to look at things because it assumes we know what another perceives of us, or even worse, we imagine that our truth may disillusion them about us.

Somehow in our belief system is the idea that if they really knew our humanness they may not like us anymore. Where do these compensations come from? Can you imagine how confusing this is for our little people who are learning the relationship between what they sense and what we teach them? They feel sadness or sense one thing on an energy level and when they ask us "Are you sad?" the response is "of course not, I'm fine," because we don't want to burden them with adult problems. Just because we admit we are sad doesn't mean we have to go into an explanation with a toddler, but we can be honest and confirm their perceptions. Instead, we end up burdening them with the dilemma of reconciling what they sense to be truth from their internal guidance, with what we tell them is truth, from our response to them. It is through innocent interactions such as these that we become conditioned to turn off trusting our feelings and our perceptions, and in turn adopt the idea that to be true to ourselves in actions and communications with others, we will disillusion them about us. We create the habit of telling half-truths to try and bridge the gap between gaining acceptance and our need to be understood.

When we experience chaos in our lives, it is a good indication that there are several subconscious programs acting through us, in unawareness. To bring our focus internally, and allow our internal state to guide us to the subconscious programs, we are opening the doorway for Spirit to enter our awareness, and bring us back to the truth within. With this truth realized, we are reunited with our natural state of clarity, where we see things for what they are. In realigning ourselves from within, we automatically disassociate with all that has resonated with our subconscious perceptions, creating confusion and chaos in response to our current conscious perceptions.

Have you had the experience of consciously choosing to heal, only to find that everything around you seems to fall apart, and you are plummeted into confusion and doubts that had never entered your experience before? Nothing makes sense to us just before we make a breakthrough in bringing awareness to an active aspect of Self that has been completely unrecognized. In that moment of not knowing anything, we are released from our held perceptions and shown clarity. Chaos symbolizes the internal battle between the conscious "will" to maintain order, and the subconscious aspect of Self, struggling to be heard, through the busyness of all the other energies, being attracted to the mental plane. Through the subtle senses, our body can lead us from the busyness of the mental plane, to the wisdom being expressed through our physical structure.

RESPONSIVENESS TO SELF

There is a warning that goes along with the development of awareness on the conscious level. With Conscious Awareness comes responsibility. I can't stress enough that the Process of Inner Alchemy is done in Sacred Space. Our thoughts and perceptions belong to our private world for most of us unless we choose to share them. This is not actually the highest truth, as we are energetic beings and those with highly developed intuition see and feel our energy, the same as we see someone's clothes as they walk down the street. We wear our whole story, the intimate, the public, our relationship to others, our perceptions of the world, and our state of disease, are all in our field of energy. So, it is a bit disconcerting to realize that in actuality we all live in glass houses. For those of us who are Self-conscious this is really unraveling! With this realization is also a good reason to start busting yourself on the things you think and do that you would have a hard time standing by if called on! The saying, " Do unto others as you would have them do unto you" has great truth to it. Busting ourselves is a good exercise in humility, because it keeps integrity with our intentions, and honesty of our own humanness in turn gives integrity to our perceptions of another.

The reality is that even though everyone's mind is able to perceive everything at all levels, few have developed the ability to use their mind on all levels in conscious awareness. And those that have developed their abilities extensively have come to respect the privacy, and honor for Self and another, that comes with using these gifts. As our awareness increases we naturally relate to people's energy as instinctually as we feel someone when we give them a hug. To intuitively engage at this deeper level of awareness is to place focus on our own resistance to accepting them as they are expressing themselves from the deeper goodness within them. But to delve into intuitively perceiving specific information about an individual, with respect and integrity of their part in the process, requires their conscious consent. To specifically follow their energy to the source within them as the observer, the recorder of what the body is expressing in its subtle energy is different than being present in the moment with them. Inevitably, intuitive input will be misunderstood as personal opinion if not defined as to the source of it. Have we not all had the experience of sharing our true feelings in the moment with someone only to have them tell us what it means and what we should do? This is a very good way to separate oneself from being received even if the intent is authentically to be helpful. To engage with intuitive information is *never* in the form of what is right for someone to do, as that is a personal interpretation of information another expresses, whether it be energetic in origin or not. It is natural that anyone learning to work with their intuition comes to experience this in their eagerness to help others, believing they have something to offer to illuminate another. To believe we have the ability to illuminate another, in itself is a big illusion we all need to overcome in embracing humility, but a necessary one if we are to transform barriers into acceptance. Just as someone may not be aware of our abilities, we may in turn not be aware of their own developed abilities! Assumptions can take us further from receiving another in their truth because we have negated to truly attend to what they communicate to us.

 The opportunity offered in a situation may best be realized sometimes by having the courage to openly jump in with enthusiasm, and staying with it, until clarity reveals itself through honestly revealing our perceptions to others. To remember to be gentle with our selves as we uncover our own misconceptions, and recognize that there is no greater teacher, than experience its Self. We are all students of life in every moment and taking responsibility for own our perceptions opens us to receive others as they really are with greater clarity, not as we have assumed them to be, through our own experience of Self.

RECOGNIZING THE LANGUAGE OF THE SOUL

Our Intuitive sensing is like listening to a foreign language when we first start working with it. When we stop trying to translate each word into meaning for us, and begin feeling the intonation of the sounds and the flow of the delivery we start to get a jist of its meaning through the feeling within us. The difference between learning a new language and working intuitively is that using intuition is a remembering of the language of the Soul, which has been with us forever. To hear the language of the Soul is an inner listening through feeling completely with our being. Intuition is the sensing that leads to the truth of the Soul that we all recognize and know once connecting with it. The more we learn to listen with our hearts to our subtle senses, the more we begin to understand it as a deep and profound knowing. Working with the levels of perception, we are led into the awareness that each one of these levels can reveal to us. The more we attend, the more receptive we become to subtle energy, and we gain faith in feeling safe to go deeper with our sensing.

It is in the moment of just stopping in our tracks, becoming still and listening to our heart, that we take the leap of faith to stand suspended in the place of knowing nothing. It is to be courageous enough to just remain in this place of knowing nothing, without any preconceived ideas about what is being expressed, that the truth is revealed in its simplicity to us through the body energy. There is no mistaking the validity of the sensing because when we look around us in our physical environment, wherever we are in that moment, there is something that shows us this very thing in an ordinary way we can relate to within the context of our current experience. It has been there before us in something that we see everyday but our awareness reveals so much more about it to us. The gift can be realized through this process of opening to greatness. It's like rereading a book we read a few years previous and even though we are reading the same words, they have so much more meaning to us. Even though the words are the same, our ability to understand them in their deeper meaning has grown.

Through the journey within, applying the Process of Inner Alchemy, we become humbled by our conscious thoughts and enter the realm of reverence to the power of Soul to communicate through the aspects of Self, its true needs to us. Just as we come to appreciate the depth that is within a written message as we grow in our own understanding and experience, so does our appreciation of common names and descriptions we have been exposed to describe the world of energy. There are a few misconceptions about intuition and working with energy that can be misleading, and foster resistance for us in venturing near them. Several words, or phrases, I hear used frequently have caused me to wonder where they come from, except in attempt to keep ourselves feeling safe in a fear based reality. As with everything there are many ways to perceive the same thing, so I offer the following as an exploration of the possible positive polarities that can exist in our personal perceptions of working with Energy.

The following are my perceptions coming from a reality I perceive as demonstrating mutual honor, trust, respect and love. A reality, based on these virtues, supports being true to actualizing all aspects of Self, and aligning with the truth of who we really are, as Souls.

CLEARING ENERGY

Energy is timeless and is in constant motion by its nature. For energy to change from one state of experience to another for us it must transform through our perceptions. Energy does not disappear because by its nature it cannot; it can only appear to disappear to us. Where there is negative energy present it's polar opposite in the form of positive energy also exists. To clear energy, as most refer to it, is to take what is negative and remove it from the area it has collected to alleviate discomfort on some level of experience. There is initial relief experienced but the root of the imbalance can only be changed if it is balanced through realization of its polarity, a positive energy. Therefore in clearing the negative energy without realizing the positive energy, the negative energy will recollect in that area in response to the attraction still present. The attraction being the retained belief or thought that we have yet to realize in its polarity.

Think of an area in the body that has a collection of negative energy where we feel pain, and apply the concept of our Sensitivity, a positive energy, being encapsulated by this equally negative energy to balance it. Would removing the negative energy assure that the positive would be experienced if it were free to express itself? What if there is a belief, a specific thought, or decision to disengage from our Sensitivity, that serves to separate it from our consciousness even if we remove the negative charge? Unless we address the belief or conscious choice, as it exists subconsciously, the negative energy will re-collect in response to holding that Sensitivity separate from our awareness. To take from another what is within their power to heal themselves if exposed in its truth has a limited effect. It is misleading to think that we can clear energy when in actuality we can move or transform it, but it is and always will exist in our perceptions as polarities as long as it is not actualized. As individuals we must choose what is right for us from a place of awareness, so we can choose to free the limited perception so it may be part of our Wholeness not held separate. In liberating our perception from its subconscious state, we are once again reunited with our Sensitivity that was encapsulated within the confines of the negative energy. The illusion is revealed and we once again may embrace the Sensitivity as a virtue rather than a source of pain and separation from others. If we come to free the positive polarity in a state of awareness, then it is not collected in one place, it is in harmony and working with the whole. The negative also is present as part of that whole and free to move so its not collected to create discomfort.

How would we know the light if we did not come to know the darkness and have the experience of relationship with them? They both exist always. One cannot exist without the other, nor would we wish them to, because with both we are able to experience the full spectrum of truth as it exists in all experience.

PROTECTING OURSELVES

This I am going to put into the context of protecting ourselves from negative energy. Many energetic teachings place focus on learning to protect ones Self from the effects of negative energy. This one perception alone, in my eyes, is responsible for many 'Energy Workers' becoming sick when working with others. The only way that negative energy can affect us, or hurt us, is if within ourselves we carry a frequency that resonates with it. Many people invest a great amount of energy in putting in place measures to protect themselves from negative energy. This act alone is a symptom of our belief that negative energy is a threat to our safety. Inside us there is a buried Sensitivity we have yet to unveil, and as such we are not empowered to recognize the Sensitivity in another that has shown its True Self to us.

So when we feel the effects of negative energy or resonate with a symptom someone around us is exhibiting we have a part of our

Self that is yearning to be recognized and healed, so the Sensitivity connected to our Soul may be liberated into its freeform again. To transform the part that sticks with us is not only to heal an aspect of Self, but also the opportunity to liberate a thought, or belief, that no longer serves us in a fuller experience of who we are. When we take responsibility for the part of the negative energy that has resonated with us, not only have we healed our Self, but we also have been given the gift to see beyond that aspect of negativity in another to their Sensitivity in its power of goodness. To believe another has the ability or power to hurt us in an illusion, and it serves only to occupy and invest our energy in protecting ourselves. Being 'out there' with who we are exposes us to all that has potential to help heal us. Where we are unable to see a positive potential in others is an indication within ourselves we have yet to realize our own potential. Our negative perceptions of others can bring awareness to what is unconsciously within oneself through mirroring our own limitations in accepting another as they are.

ENERGY NEVER LIES

There may be many facts, circumstances and numbers of believers that support certain ideas. If what we are told and what we feel don't jive, follow the feelings or sensations within before buying into believing what is being presented to us. There is a misperception somewhere. As we come to recognize being triggered, we can track the sensation to its origin to release our limitation, or the idea itself may be limited from our experience. Or it can be the presentation of the information is possibly not authentic with the intent behind it, and within us we are sensing the inconsistency. When someone is not telling the truth, or withholding their truth, their energy feels different than the message they are consciously giving. We don't believe them at some level. This is also an excellent tool to start busting ourselves on bad habits we have developed to deliver our truth. Many of us come up with ways to make our needs known by finding ways to deliver them, we believe will be more acceptable to others, and believe that they are more likely to respond to, rather than honestly stating them. We tend to operate with agenda's we don't even recognize, not because we think we are deceivers, but because we haven't consciously identified our true needs. Energy never lies - people unfortunately do to protect themselves. When we know the truth we can always heal. It is much better, even if we experience hurt, to have another's truth upfront, because we have the ability to acknowledge our own truth in response to it. When another's truth is hidden or not acknowledged honestly, we can spend years living without our Sensitivity that got buried with the hurt of the miscommunication.

In developing our subtle senses we begin resonating with our external world more clearly as well. Food shopping in awareness can help us discern what is healthy for our bodies and what is not. Labels do not always list what is inside a product. There are ingredients that manufacturers tell us are harmless but our bodies have a negative response to them. The packaging and information conveyed through the marketing of many products gives the intellect an idea about the product. If we are to invest in our health, our happiness and peace within, we are maybe better to place integrity with how we resonate with what is presented to us in many circumstances, not just in people, but products and services as well. In breaking free of our own internal deceptions, we are empowered to break free of what is presented to feel within if there is actual threat or just perceived threat in what we ingest and endorse in our external environment. The practices that are used in making products, the marketing of products, the labor used to bring the product to market, and the product itself as ecologically beneficial can all be felt through the energy of that product as you pick it up off the market shelf to buy. The product may not have life itself, but it carries the energy of everything that has touched it.

LETTING GO

When facing a challenge in our lives it is often suggested that we just *let go* of whatever we are holding onto. I don't think any of us consciously really want to hold onto a negative emotion, ailment or an unpleasant perception we have of our current situation. What is it that we have to *let go* of anyway? The current subconscious belief or perception is possibly keeping us from realizing the full potential of ourselves, but letting go gives us the idea we have to get rid of something. Maybe it is the limitation itself we have to relinquish rather than the perception itself. To expand on a currently held perception would possibly allow a fuller realization of truth. Often it is very difficult to define the perception, or belief we are operating from, in context to our current experience, because it is not in awareness that we chose it. The more we try not to think about it and rise above it, the further suppressed our true feelings or perceptions become because we think they are not acceptable, which they aren't to us, but we are at a loss to resolve them in their current context. They niggle away at us, and even though we know they are there, we pretend to others and ultimately ourselves that they are wrong to have, so we ignore and dissociate from them. We've already made a judgment about the perceptions we have of ourselves in the current state of experience without really hearing or acknowledging them in their truth. To take our current experience and intuitively listen to our bodies, through acknowledgement of our emotions and then our body sensations, we have the ability to find understanding as to their significance for us. So the act of *letting go* is actually the act of *embracing* our limited aspect of Self at a level that can elevate the perception into a greater understanding. To *let go* requires *coming back* to accepting our True Self and the expanding of perceptions that can better serve us in our potential to heal. We don't really *let go* of anything- we break free of the limitation the current perception provides and *bring it back* to fuller awareness.

ANGER

Anger represents one of the most powerful, and potentially empowering emotions we have been blessed with. When we learn to listen to our bodies intuitively, the energy of anger presents itself through sensation within us long before it becomes explosive. The energy of anger is unmistakable but many of us have never come to realize it until it comes firing through our emotions in the conscious state. Expressed as emotion it can be devastating to be on the receiving end of it. Anger as a sensation is a welling up, like a peacock sensing an intruder. It is a signal within us that whatever is happening at that moment in our experience is in complete contradiction to a core belief or value that we hold and it is hurting us. To embrace anger when it first emerges in the form of energy is an opportunity to stop and listen to our heart so we can remain in line with our True Self and respond with our own truth from a place of strength rather than feeling threatened. Misunderstanding by another fuels anger in us, and maintains it in its destructive polarity. It is helpful to remind ourselves that as great as anger can be, beneath it there is love of the same magnitude that is being concealed by hurt. To recognize the hurt in another that evokes such an expression of anger from them is to take the situation into a conscious awareness that understanding can be achieved and love be experienced through listening with our heart, not their words. Is it possible that their Soul is guiding them to trust us to take that current expression and see through it to the hurt within them yearning to be recognized? Anger is a symptom of separation from our True Self. Coming from our heart takes the threat of being hurt out of the equation because it endorses what intuition can reveal to us in a greater truth. Honesty with our Self and others is the key to opening ourselves to the language of the heart with one another.

THE FACETS OF MIND

Our mind has many facets. To learn the difference in the energy of each facet is to become confident in what the mind is showing us about ourselves. Our current perceptions are not a threat; they are a means in which we can recognize something is not right for us. If we don't feel good, or see the beauty and gift a situation offers us to experience, it is an aspect of Self that is not working in harmony with what we know in the true knowledge of our Soul.

Our mind is our greatest tool and has the ability to guide and liberate our experience of Self in its many expressions. To place trust in our mind is to place faith in our highest good because without limitation, our mind can reveal all levels of experience in their multi-dimensional states. The mind is all encompassing and takes in everything on all levels whether we are consciously aware of what is going on or not. Our mind is the only thing we do have control over and to become familiar with its abilities is to take responsibility to create the experience we choose. We always have the choice of what and how we choose to perceive ourselves. Thoughts we don't like can be tracked to their origins within us to be liberated into a fuller truth. There are many thoughts we did not consciously choose to adopt and once having brought our awareness to what doesn't feel good to us we have the ability to recognize them, source them to their origin, and in turn liberate them into a truer expression of who we are as Soul. To work with mind is to place faith in our innate goodness again, and in turn resonate with the goodness in others.

Our mind is the faithful recorder. To consciously work with mind is genius. Any deceptions are because of OUR intentions, conscious or unconscious. Being honest with ourselves is to approach situations without preconceived ideas about what will be shown to us. To catch ourselves playing games helps place integrity in our minds ability to show us truth, and the part we play in giving it integrity. Becoming aware of our selves in all aspects of our life, and consciously bringing awareness to our perceptions and what they are revealing to us about our limitations, is to open the doors to a world that also has the ability to show us unlimited possibilities for the experience of love, peace and joy for us all.

CHOICES

How many of us have a hard time making decisions? Not just about the big things in life, but even the little things, like what to wear today or what color to paint the living room wall. When we have a hard time making decisions it is because we either don't have all the facts or we have not determined what is important to us. We are lacking information on some level and are being pulled in many directions not wanting to make a mistake because there is something missing on one end of the spectrum between what we are presented externally and what we feel internally. Those of us who have no problem making decisions know what is important to our True Self and it becomes simple to take what is presented externally as resonating or not resonating with what supports and expresses our internal truth of who we are.

Choosing what to wear stems from knowing who we are and choosing how we wish to carry that expression into the experience of that day. We wish to support being comfortable with who we are in various situations. If we place our focus on the situation we are entering that day, then it is more difficult to choose what expression we are most comfortable with based on external acceptance. To be true to our Soul, we choose what is right for us at this time. The awareness of True Self takes the emphasis off what we think we are supposed to choose, and places it with knowing what we choose for our Self. Choices that become difficult signal that our criteria for choosing has been based on trying to please external criteria rather than honesty with the internal truth of what is important to us at the level of True Self. We are making choices constantly everyday whether we realize it or not, so whether we start up the stairs with the left foot or right foot is a decision at some level. Bringing awareness to what we automatically do each day can also be very revealing to the underlying programs we are running on. Our subconscious mind is showing itself through our actions all the time is we stop and take notice!

CONFUSION

This is really the experience of not knowing what to choose. It is also a very good sign that a shift in perception is required in order to move ahead with clarity with the part of our Self that is not in harmony with our Soul. To find ourselves in the midst of confusion is a huge red flag that signals we are making a choice unconsciously. We may be sabotaging True Self without realizing it. To stop and observe what thoughts we have going through our minds may reveal we are focusing on meeting external criteria, versus internal criteria. We may be focusing on what experience we DON'T want to have, versus what experience we DO want to have. To bring our focus into awareness is to work hand in hand with what our mind can bring into our awareness that supports the magnificence of Soul. Often, we focus on what we don't want to experience, without realizing it, and in doing so we subconsciously filter out perceiving everything that supports what we DO want to experience. We actually create that which we most dread by bringing into our awareness all the choices that support what we don't want to have happen to us. Our fears become endorsed by the experience we create for ourselves. Part of us wants assurance and a sense of safety, so we want to cross all the bridges of the experience before we even get there. We end up placing our focused thoughts on our fears unconsciously and in so doing we filter out all that exists that doesn't resonate with our fears. We miss everything that could support a positive outcome, as it does not exist to us consciously with these filters in place.

This is how we have learned to keep ourselves feeling safe, but it is serving to keep us where we are, not where we deserve to be in our freedom of expression. Confusion is our way of expressing that we are not able to be clear with ourselves. We all get confused and it is frustrating because it feeds all the ideas we have about ourselves that we are not good enough, not intelligent or quick enough to grasp concepts, and most importantly that we will make the wrong choice. The frustration amplifies all of our self-doubts and fears of failure. Confusion can be GREAT, if we learn to recognize what it represents, by bringing focus to the subtle energies again rather than all the old tapes of recollection. To simply focus on the moment brings integrity to what can be revealed on the part of the path we are standing on about how we really feel about something. To reconnect with what is important to us, and what we really need, not what we have come to believe we need based on others experience of fulfillment. We don't have to have everything figured out ahead of time, because to be connected with our intuitive abilities is to become the innocent child open to receive through the eyes of wonderment as if experiencing the part of the path we find ourselves on for the first time. Making mistakes is not to be dreaded, but accepted as essential to learning about what outcomes are possible based on our choices. Through the child's eyes in innocence, there is no such thing as a mistake. It is the feeling of disappointing those we respect that create the impression of making mistakes, when we fail to impress them with who we are. Disappointment is difficult to achieve if we are open with our thoughts and feelings for others to know us as we really are. We are full of goodness as who we really are… the disappointment can only be a reflection of their own inability to be connected to their own humanness. And impressions come from something out of the ordinary happening. People, and events that stand out from what we expect makes impressions on us all. Nothing would ever change if we didn't allow for the unexpected and embrace what we learn from the impression it made on us, be it good or bad. We are always free to change our minds and make different choices when we become aware we are making them.

COMPASSION

I hear the word compassion often spoken by many spiritual and aware people, but I didn't really understand what it meant because as they spoke to me, I didn't feel good. I came away feeling very misunderstood and righteous about what I believed, because I felt that I hadn't been recognized for who I was. They couldn't hear me where I was, because they had already decided where I was by my circumstance, and had interpreted it for me. When I did speak, I didn't feel heard. I wondered if they had perceived my circumstance as one that I suffered in or that was unfortunate in some way? I never actually felt unfortunate, so in hindsight I think my pride was engaged by the assumption. All that I could hear from them at that time was that they knew more than me, which was probably true, but their attempt to share their knowledge did not move me to find more within myself. Instead, their dialogue further separated me from accepting their wisdom. I admit I can be very willful sometimes, so maybe they were being compassionate and I couldn't accept or receive the value in their advice. To me, there was an exchange missing, and it just didn't feel right for me. I wasn't moved to feel any better about myself through their defining my problem to me, or what I needed to do, based on their interpretation. I heard many a "you should…" from people when Harrison was an infant.

Just as God had posed a dilemma in my acceptance of myself, I decided to redefine compassion. I noticed that the same feeling overcame me when I heard the words "compassion," and "you should." Both were evoking this righteous streak and I had developed the compensation of Self-reliance from very early on in my life without even knowing it as a result. This very Self-reliance that was now working against me, had enabled me to experience success in many aspects of my life up until this point. Through Inner Alchemy, I worked through the layers of compensations and limitations that were now keeping me from moving forward. All I had was a feeling that was uncomfortable from these words, that is all I knew. I was blind to what was going on from a deeper level. Through intuition, I came to understand that my Self-reliance had ultimately proven to isolate me from placing faith in others to really love me for who I am. I was trusting Self, but I was missing faith in my Essence as Soul to be worthy of love, not for what I did, or knew, but for being true to who I am, outwardly, in all expressions of Self. It becomes very easy to think that what we have come to discover as our truth is going to be what another still has to discover about their truth. The truth is always within us, but do we resonate with it as an aspect of Self, or an aspect in another, without getting past that to experience the Whole of another and ourselves. How do we know unless we can really hear them in clarity? Or more to the point, can we hear in another what we are deaf to within ourselves? I obviously didn't understand compassion back then because I was experiencing it as feeling patronized and insignificant. Others weren't the problem, nor were "compassion" or "what I should do." They were just triggers trying to get my attention to something important I needed to liberate inside me.

Remember my story about going to Spain to teach Medical Intuition for the first time? What became my conscious experience with authority in Spain, had been trying to show itself to me since childhood through a subconscious belief about my own worthiness. I knew leaving that experience in Spain that the process had been initiated in working with my own wisdom, but I had no idea that where I was being led had anything to do with worthiness. With this adopted belief unrecognized, I missed really valuable advice and authentic support that was being offered repeatedly to me throughout my life. It's as if I made life harder than it needed to be, without even knowing it. I repeatedly unknowingly attracted the " know it all aspect" in other people that repeatedly evoked this streak of Self-reliance in me because somewhere inside I believed I wasn't worthy of their support, because I would never measure up to their expectations. I subconsciously believed everyone must know more than me. All this did was further fuel my desire to be Self-reliant in hopes of proving my ability to be worthy, my own way, because I trusted myself.

To function from Self, isolated from the higher truths of Soul, can create a misconception of who we are. Our perceptions through unrealized Self can lead us into believing that what is true for one is true for all of us, in the *same* way. Love has many expressions, and to decide what is right or wrong, black or white in any situation or personal perception is to place our Self in the position to judge where another stands, in their current position, in relation to our experience. We completely miss the subtle yearning of the Soul to be heard in its power, to transform our limited perceptions of Self, into greater awareness of our being.

For me, compassion has come to mean, believing in another to find for themselves their greatest truth, because we see past current circumstance, to embrace the infinite light within. Seeing another through the eyes of love, knowing they have within them the resources and ability to heal if they can come to see themselves through the eyes of love as well. Compassion was always going to be just out of my grasp of understanding, until I realized the Essence of love within my own being. To help unveil this within us, or to experience this in one another, becomes possible through the mutual exchange of acceptance and receptiveness. Listening with the heart can bring this depth to relationship with others. Through the heart, we are moved past engaging an aspect of Self out of reaction, separate from Soul, into aligning an aspect of Self with Soul, through responsiveness to another. It is hard to open to the Sensitivity of the Soul with another without feeling received and accepted by them for who we are.

Compassion originates from the level of Soul, which is our Essence in its magnificence, and it reflects the magnificence in others to us when we are connected to our own. If we hold Sacred Space for another we come to appreciate their truth, and using intuition to hear what our body is revealing on a deeper level can endorse our internal resources to reconnect with another's magnificence, rather than what may be assumed by their circumstance. A disease state is *one* aspect of Self, which has been unrecognized by us, in its limitation. There are many other aspects within us that we have come to know in a fuller more enlightened state of awareness. To be assessed by another, on this one aspect that is having trouble, can feel like a great injustice. All the other aspects within us *can* have the ability to help liberate the one separate aspect to be aligned with Soul, if engaged through compassion. In turn, there is fuller experience brought to all the other aspects of Self as well, because they are all connected to the Soul. Sacred Space is a safe environment where the vibration of compassion is held to facilitate meeting challenges with support, because we know others are magnificent and able to do it if they are reminded of their Soul's perfection.

The trusted Source of knowledge becomes internally validated through the Process of Inner Alchemy. Knowledge others offer can be consciously chosen to facilitate and support the resources and integrity within us already cultivated, from this level of awareness.

The Encarta World English Dictionary defines Compassion as *sympathy for the suffering of others, often including a desire to help.*

With the ability to incorporate our greater senses of intuition such a definition seems limiting, as it seems to be aligned with separation from another, in that *suffering* is what is perceived. It implies that the perceived sufferer is alone. If it is another's suffering that we perceive, is it possible that within ourselves, it is our own suffering that seeks liberation as well? The circumstance defines the person instead of the person having the resources or attracting the resources that can liberate them from circumstance. We are not our circumstance; we are who we are within a circumstance. Situations change depending on how we are able to act from our inner resources to become liberated from our circumstance through awareness. Through awareness, the available external resources may be recognized and accepted that will facilitate our liberation from unfortunate circumstance, when validation comes from our internal awareness. We are unable to recognize or receive help offered by others sometimes because we have not yet realized or identified our true needs to our Self. When we feel sympathy for another, is it because we are unable to perceive the potential within them, which has the ability to liberate them from unfortunate circumstance?

Mother Theresa, to me, was an amazing beacon of compassion. Through her complete presence, she *was* compassion, in her power to transform suffering into peace. We can't change circumstance to liberate the innocent unless we can somehow transform the suffering with a deeper recognition of the beauty and peace of the Soul that has been silenced. From this truth of the heart and Soul, it becomes easy to know how to be there for another regardless of circumstance because there is love that unites us, rather than suffering. All of our resources internal and external become shared, from the pool of greater knowledge, where we are Soul. Unfortunate circumstance ceases to exist, as it is merely a perception that keeps us further separated from resources that can liberate our bodies, and our environment, to better reflect the beauty of the Soul that inhabits it.

THE ASPECTS OF SELF IN RELATION TO TRUE SELF

In relation to the work of Inner Alchemy, the aspects of Self represent where we have segmented the experience of Self in order to help define its relationship with our Soul. An aspect of Self aligned with Soul becomes True Self, as Self is actualized, it goes beyond what collectively we have defined, to become a unique expression of who we are as Soul. With True Self emerges the potential of Soul to be realized through the conscious mind. With the inception of the archetype concept, by the Swiss psychiatrist Carl Gustav Jung, a structure was born that enabled us to define the parts of our Self that needed analysis in order to better understand ourselves in relation to Soul and the collective unconscious. With my work with the Process of Inner Alchemy, I am suggesting that we take a step beyond analysis through our mental state alone and redefine our Self by intuitively sensing, what these aspects have to share with us in their individual expression subconsciously within us. Using the Process of Inner Alchemy we are consciously embarking on discovering the subconsciously active aspects of our Self and recognizing their unique influence on our current experience. During an Inner Alchemy session it is not important whether or not we name the aspect of Self, as the significance is not in its name but rather the recognition of the unconscious perception of our Self and the decision made about Self that serves to limit a fuller current experience of who we are.

The aspects of Self are representations of how we experience ourselves through the development of our collective unconscious. One of the most important contributions by Carl Jung to our understanding of the human psyche is the concept of the archetypes. Archetypes are primordial, unlearned aspects of the psyche, which are drawn from the collective unconscious. They are not who we are in Wholeness but rather the segments of our being that we have come to experience in relationship with our True Self. True Self is when an aspect is fully actualized in its polarities to act in unison with our Soul. As we develop in the human form we develop on the psychic level as well through the actualization of these aspects of Self. When we are born we are in Essence Selfless, as we have not developed specifically our individuality so therefore there are no active aspects of Self we have come to experience or recognize. We are one with all at birth and it is through our development physically, mentally and emotionally, that we come to develop various aspects of Self to serve our individual and collective experience.

INTEGRATING THE LEVELS OF EXPERIENCE

There are many aspects of Self that we come to find balance with through the journey of Self-actualization. Certain roles, certain situations, and certain relationships bring forth specific collective aspects of Self to be personally realized. As long as the specific aspect that is active is working in harmony with our conscious and subconscious beliefs and values we are aligned with Soul. For example, the role of mother, if aligned with Soul, goes beyond what we have come to believe "mother" is supposed to represent, into a fuller, more authentic expression of who we are when summoned in the role as a mother. It is when one of these unrealized aspects is triggered by our experience in a situation, or of another person, that we are pulled out of alignment and the opportunity to heal that which separates us from the experience of Soul is brought to our attention. So simply, to identify these unbalanced aspects of Self is to acknowledge when we don't feel good about something. So, it's not being a mother that poses the problem, rather the ideas we hold about what mother is supposed to be, that keeps us from embracing the truth of that aspect of Self, for ourselves. When our truth is embraced, this aspect will naturally come forward when the situation calls for this part of us to be engaged. The aspect within us that is "mother" goes far beyond actually giving birth to children or raising a family. The "mother" aspect within us all is the part of us that cares for and nurtures another.

It is often in the moment of recognition that we don't feel good about ourselves that we open the door to the possibility that there is something we need to heal within, so we can once again be in our center. It is in our center that we step beyond the idea we previously held about our Self, and a fuller, truer expression is liberated. In the case of the mother aspect, we step past what we have held as a reference for how this aspect is expressed into the realm of authentically bringing who we are to the role. Learning to identify what part of us has become engaged can be difficult, unless we come to recognize the various characteristics of the aspects of Self, and how we have come to express them. These aspects are commonly experienced expressions of who we are by the collective unconscious. Our personal experience of them is our individuality and to learn to recognize them is to come to work consciously with developing and understanding them within the context of our True Self. It is through this journey of Self-actualization, the realization of Self as we choose to express it, that we begin consciously work with the multi-dimensions of our perceptions. These aspects are mere reflections of how we see ourselves in our reality and can serve to show us our limitations of perception and areas that awareness can enrich our experience. They can reveal our illusions and snap us out of our drama and perception of our current experience if we choose to see them in honesty and clarity and then symbolically as they relate to the collective unconscious. To learn to work in relation to what exists as a collective unconscious, in awareness, is to liberate the limitations of these expressions into a fuller understanding and expression of who we really are in relation to the potential of our Soul.

# PART SIX:

Integrating the Feminine

THE WORLD IS WITHIN US

When we are working with healing our physical, mental and emotional bodies, to work intuitively, is to acknowledge our unconscious state of experience and our unique way of perceiving and expressing what is not in balance for us in our experience of Self. To define an aspect of Self by a name initially gives us boundaries to help define our perceptions, but it is limited as it negates the individual's perceptions of their unique experience. To create relationship with the unconscious experience requires tools that can be used to assess the unknown on the level of subtle energy. The tools already exist within us, unrealized in our unconscious, therefore we are being moved more than ever to embrace our natural resources within. The realization of these inner resources will be marked by the outward manifestation of advancements in technology, health care, education, and in all the resourceful solutions to challenges that we face in our physical environment, but it begins with understanding that we are the creators not the victims of circumstance. Much of what we are witnessing in our world in concrete terms today with the destruction of our natural resources of water, trees and air are a mere reflection of what we are experiencing in our internal world of disease with our separation from True Self. To learn how to care for our Self through awareness of our true needs, we can in turn come to recognize what is needed to care for our earth in her need to maintain balance that sustains our well being. We are not separate from our earth, our moon, our stars, our sun, or any other living being. To continue to function with this delusion that we are separate is to feed the state of disease within our own thinking as individuals and collectively. This delusion of separateness serves only to help us feel justified in not accepting responsibly for what we have been part of creating through our everyday choices.

INDIVIDUALIZED MEDICINE

With the Process of Inner Alchemy we are not leaving our mental capabilities behind, we are expanding their abilities to perceive with greater depth that which the mind can reveal through intuition. To be able to follow the energy found in the individual's body is to allow them to personally experience consciously in the now, what they had previously experienced in its original state that served to separate them from the experience of Wholeness. If we are not careful we can fall into the trap of merely naming the active aspects, which fails to fully *understand* how that individual uniquely has experienced himself or herself in a particular situation. We truly enter the realm of Individualized Medicine when we place integrity with the wisdom found at the source of the person's state of disease through Intuitive sensing. This is the part of healing that requires the human touch, in the form of our subtle senses, for there are no diagnostic machines at present able to replace or emulate the Sensitivity of an individual. Just as babies don't thrive without being touched and loved, as adults we need to feel love to thrive as well. To be able to receive love, we need to be able to re-establish integrity with True Self. This is very difficult when we have barriers within ourselves that are now serving to keep us apart from True Self and in turn our ability to be contributing to our relationship with the world we are part of. If we come to reclaim the parts of our Self that have come to separate us from the experience of Wholeness it becomes a reality to once again reclaim our relationship with our natural resources both internally and externally that create

Wholeness for us individually and for us all as a global community.

THE YIN & YANG OF SELF

The yin represents the feminine energy and the yang represents the masculine energy. Each of us is made up of both of these polarities. The yin cannot exist without the yang, just as the positive can not exist without the negative, light without dark, or male without female. The yin is the feminine energy that is sensitive, nurturing, supportive, and all encompassing by nature. It is this receptive feminine energy that is our intuition. The yang is the willful masculine energy, directed, assertive, disciplined and forceful. Some of us are more yang in our exterior expression and yin in our internal experience and vise versa. This is not to say that all men display yang energy on the exterior and/or that women display yin energy on the exterior. A yang exterior/yin interior person tends to be more assertive and forthright naturally in their outward expression of themselves and yet inside they are have extreme Sensitivity. A yin exterior/yang interior person tends to be very soft, receptive and unobtrusive in their outward expression of themselves but can be very strong and willful internally.

 Imagine you are standing outside looking up at the moon in the still of night. It is very easy to gaze at the moon because its light is soft and inviting and as you gaze at it you feel it draw you into itself. As the moon draws you in you can feel your body relax and there is peacefulness that envelops you. This sensation of warmth and comfort is the Essence of the feminine energy. As the moon is yin in nature, it draws you in because in its receptivity there is comfort in being with it. Once you are drawn in by this feminine energy you feel the strength and power of the moon's energy as it nourishes and fills you with peace. Now imagine you are outside on a bright sunny day and you look up towards the sun, which is yang in nature. It is very difficult to look directly at the sun without the need to shield your eyes. Its radiance bursts outward as if it pushes you back from getting too close or penetrating it with the naked eye. There is a force that explodes from its brilliance. If we stand with our face exposed to the sun, and close our eyes, the sensation of basking in the sun's hot rays feels glorious as it warms and invigorates us. This is the Essence of the masculine energy, and when we are open to receive it, it can inspire, it can energize and bring vitality to our experience.

Each of the aspects of Self can be expressed quite differently depending on whether we are by nature a yang exterior or a yin exterior. This is not directly related to our gender but more the natural expression of who we are and the parts of ourselves as they appear to others on the surface. An example of this would be to reflect on the aspect of the Spiritual Warrior. Depending on which type of person this aspect was expressed from it may appear to an outsider quite differently. A yang exterior person, or the Yang Spiritual Warrior, would possibly express this more vocally and assert themselves in various situations with outward expressions of enthusiasm and acts of power. Many recognize the Yang Spiritual Warrior in this type of person more noticeably than a yin exterior person. The Yin Spiritual Warrior may demonstrate this aspect of Self by becoming invisible in a crowd. Unless you were very observant and went past what was externally projected, you may miss the power within in them to sustain and nurture completely. The effects of the yang Spiritual Warrior are more visibly recognized in relation to them because they demonstrate outwardly all that matches what we physically see. Whereas the effects of the Yin Spiritual Warrior are just as visible to others, but often not recognized as relating to them because of their unassuming nature. Both these polarities of the same aspect are necessary and would not exist without the other. Both expressions have the power to transform others by being balanced in the active aspect of Self, therefore coming from our center. We naturally express our true nature differently. In other words, we bring consciousness to our natural state, by honoring what we need to be in order to be true to Self and therefore in our power. Any aspect of Self in balance is aligned with the power of transformation by its direct contact with Soul, the Source of All.

Couples have the potential to make this dynamic a living reality. One is more yang on the exterior and one is more yin on the exterior. They are naturally attracted to one another. They have the ability when true to themselves to compliment and balance each other beautifully. The relationship in conscious awareness naturally demonstrates mutual honor and respect. It is not always the woman that is the yin energy on the exterior, yet as a society this is what is commonly been accepted as their role, hence the development of an outward display of the liberation of the masculine energy that lay unrecognized internally in many women began to emerge. With the realization that we all have both the masculine and feminine qualities within us, even though the theory existed for some time, through experience, came the realization that recognition of these polarities comes from *within* not from external sources. Women have made great headway at reclaiming the power of the feminine energy now that they have determined there is no fight to be won with anyone, the conflict was within all along. In women forcing their perceptions on men they were giving away their true power, and men became deaf to them, and in turn completely void of emotion and compassion for the feminine in women, as well as in themselves. Both men and women benefit from the realization that the yin and yang coexist within us both, for many men with a similar yin energy exterior have had to delve within to learn to hold their ground in the presence of yang qualities expressed by women and other men. Ultimately, there is sameness to us all and our individual external expression based on internal acknowledgment serves to support both men and women in relationship to each other.

In a supportive partnership the opportunity for growth is immense as we each serve to ignite what lay dormant in another. It is through the tension of the polarities that the aspects of Self come to be realized in their otherwise hidden polarities, and through balance and realization become integrated into True Self. We are given the opportunity in every resistance we recognize, to heal not only our personal hurts, but also the collective assumptions about these hurts. Ideally, as we reach our potential and the aspects of Self are actualized, we become more balanced in our exterior and interior polarities of yin and yang. Therefore within each of us we become the yin and the yang in balance and the masculine qualities are equally balanced by the feminine qualities. To live in the state of full realization of the active aspects of Self is to naturally bring forward the qualities that best serve the situation. There are times that to be true to ourselves and aligned with Soul we need to engage the masculine energy of standing our ground and speaking our truth with assertiveness. There are other situations that require engaging the feminine energy of listening with the heart and responding with silence in order to be received without threat. When the two qualities merge in harmony we are better at discerning how best to respond authentically and with the security within to speak our truth with kindness and compassion because we come from our Soul. From Soul we are beyond the aspects of Self and truly receive and respond from the knowledge and experience of Love.

Now, more than ever we are seeing the emergence of the feminine energy in both men and women. Many men are now becoming more comfortable expressing their feminine energy and engaging intuitively with life. Women have spent many years now exercising their masculine energy in hopes of acquiring equality with men and recognition of their contributions. Women have experienced their power in expressing the masculine energy and now are free to express the feminine without feeling intimidation or threat to their receptivity by the masculine energy. Through balancing both the yin and the yang within ourselves through experiencing them, we find security and an appreciation for these expressions in one another. Maybe now is the time we can be at peace within ourselves, and in turn one another, learn to listen with our hearts to one another, and nurture the development and expression of both the masculine and feminine energies within us all without feeling threatened.

There are situations that call forward the receptiveness of the feminine energy to be asserted and the assertiveness of the masculine energy to stand in stillness in order to receive. If we learn this balance within ourselves it becomes much easier to appreciate it in our partners. Otherwise the masculine energy becomes so focused on hearing itself, that it fails to nurture that which sustains it in clarity, the feminine energy. The feminine energy of intuition withers from meeting deaf ears and becomes isolated in its Sensitivity. This is the dynamic we have been experiencing and witnessing for some time and it isn't working for many of us. We are becoming emotionally void in our experiences and so focused on what is important to us as individuals that we fail to recognize what is important to others, and what is important to us all. Are our needs ultimately so different? Our relationships with others mirror our own duality, so what we don't recognize in awareness, further separates us from our intuition, our Sensitivity and awareness of the feminine energy, that can take us to a greater truth within ourselves and in turn a more profound relationship with another. There is great potential offered by committing to partnerships with others in awareness, as we are challenged to more fully develop ourselves.

ONENESS & WHOLENESS AS AN EVOLUTIONARY PROCESS

We begin at birth with the experience of being One with the All. Through our life experience we come to experience Self-actualization through the development of our Individuality. Through our experience of Self in its many expressions in harmony with Soul we come to experience Wholeness. The experience of Wholeness once again unites us with the experience of Oneness that returns us to the realization of Selflessness. The collective pool of consciousness ever expands as we all contribute through our expanding awareness of who we really are and our world evolves as it reflects our conscious awareness.

THE ESSENCE OF INTUITION

This feminine energy is the Essence of intuition and manifests from the wisdom within, that assures us, acknowledges our worth, sustains our Sensitivity, and nurtures resourcefulness in our contribution to life we are part of. I've named this energy the Cherished Woman because it is through my own perceptions that I came to find her. The *Cherished Woman* is the expression from within of the feminine energy connected to Soul. I came to experience her through the everyday experience of learning to trust the feminine of my True Self. When I found the Cherished Woman I came to recognize all the Cherished Women in my life who had patiently held sacred space for me to find my courage to embrace her. I believe the Cherished Woman symbolizes the sacred rite of passage that the feminine energy has to birth during one's life to experience Wholeness. The Essence of the message is about acknowledging and embracing the power of feminine energy, and holding true to what is in the heart and Soul no matter what life appears to be showing you, for it is in the depths of our being, that we find truth, without fear, of what is being asked of us to bring forward. I think that any man, or woman, who has become receptive to the feminine energy of intuition, will resonate with the stillness, the beauty, the incredible magic that surrounds us in every breath we breathe, being present with others in our life. So, I believe that for anyone who consciously connects to Soul, a similar message will emerge in Essence, but we all have a unique expression of our

Soul energy. When I sat down and wrote this I was moved as I felt her emerge, as the Cherished Woman, from my heart into words. It was the feeling of coming home, to all that is safe, knowing, and accepting of what I am and gratitude for the gifts from others that helped me find my way there. In that moment I felt complete. Returning to that feeling is the challenge that resurfaces daily, as we continue the Process of Inner Alchemy, to integrate what we know from the level of Soul into what we have become unknowingly in our present life circumstance. Life offers us this blessing in every experience we have the courage to embrace in awareness.

A Cherished Woman

Is one that stands in the middle of adversity and holds the center of sacred space.
Surrounding her are all those that are drawn to her
and depend on her energy
to bring them back to focus on what really matters.

As she stands her ground softly and confidently
she draws on the infinite resources of the great mother earth.
She has been given knowledge of all the gifts that flow from Source
so that she may display all their virtues for others to recognize.

They say that home is where the heart is.
Who tends to holding that sacred space without acknowledgment or reminding?
Who brings forward the meaning in relationship
when everything around us is fragmented and we feel alone?

It is the cherished woman,
for she has wings that are made of a feather from each of the angels.

*Her smile reminds us of her kindness and gratitude for being blessed
with the task of holding sacred space that is safe for others to be who they are.*

*She inspires, she encourages, she nurtures
what is unseen, and unnoticed by most.
She holds strong to faith that in standing in her center
she radiates truth and permeates all that keeps others from rejoicing in
their greatness.*

*Around this woman we find aspects of her in many that surround her.
She holds the symbol and vibration of love no matter what.
Their return of kindness and honor is her silent prayer answered.
It is in this moment of recognition that she becomes the cherished woman.
The cherished woman embraces the mother,
the pioneer, the inspirer, the believer, and the magnificent butterfly.
She becomes all aspects of expression when she recognizes her sacred role.*

*When she stands alone in her wisdom she serves as a beacon.
When she stands with her arms around those who need comfort she serves
as sustenance. When she speaks her truth,
those around her find courage, to find their own truth.*

*The cherished woman is the Goddess
that stands invisible in every situation.
She is visible to those that seek truth within themselves,
for it is in the depths of Self-knowledge that we first catch sight of her.*

*When we stand up within that sacred space she has courageously held for us,
we feel her,
and then we begin to see that she has been there
standing in stillness all along in the center.*

*Everyone has a cherished woman in his or her lives,
but do they know her to see her?
Remember to show her, tell her and acknowledge her with your kindness*

and honor,
as it is in this gratitude in which we find and truly experience her.

She is blessed with many gifts
and those that cherish her find they are blessed by all the angels that protect and guide her.
For it is these angels who placed the feather wings
to help those with poor vision to recognize her.

In seeking to find her you will begin to see her many aspects in those all around you.
But the cherished woman is the one who stands in the center of sacred space.
Patiently, lovingly and compassionately
holding the vibration until others decide to join her...

It is at that moment that she spreads her wings with joy at having become fulfilled.
She may now give herself permission to experience Wholeness,
for she has given birth to many expressions of life's bountiful gifts
that in turn too become cherished.

-Alison Feather Adams-

Acknowledgements

*T*hese people have appeared as angels on my path, and although I didn't recognize the significance of their appearance in its entirety at the time, I have come to appreciate through my own growth how profound their presence has been in igniting the truth within me.

Thank you Mikhael, Kate, Harrison and Alex for being my family and greatest teachers. You have grounded me, you have loved me unconditionally, and you have repeatedly proven to me that working with energy is simple, authentic and always tells the truth. Most importantly, you have loved me the way I am, and walked hand in hand with me through the creation of what you find in these pages.

I am grateful to my Yaya and my Mom for being cherished women long before I realized their sacred roles. The woman with grace and the gift of friendship in my life has been Tricia Secretan. Not only are you a wonderful friend with a magnificent spirit, but you have also been a voice that has inspired me, and kept me out of my head, and in my heart, where I hear clearly. Thank you Elsse Dorbeck, my Godmother, for leaving the artist's impression on me as a child, with flowers, poetry and books about Fairies.

It was with Don Augustin Rivas-Vasquez, the Peruvian Ayahuasca Shaman, that I opened to life's possibilities and experienced profound healing. The first Qigong I ever learned was with Bernie Bayard, a great teacher and healer, who encouraged me to find clarity through my heart. My heart found Mikhael, my husband, so I am most grateful for his shared wisdom. I became a student of Sheng Zhen Wuji Yuan Gong with Master Li Jun Feng, also on Bernie's advice. And gratitude goes beyond words to Sonya Visser, our office manager, for showing up each day with a smile and hug for all the angels in ordinary clothes that bless our office each day. It is with deep gratitude to my patients, for bringing clarity to the profound transformation possible, through the Process of Inner Alchemy.

Thank you Anita Wintels, for your courage and dedication to working with me. Amidst reading and rereading copy as the process of committing language to print unfolded for me, you have kept my faith intact for openly being who I am. Janet Percival, Laurie Simmonds, Anita, and Tricia, your sincere and honest feedback was a great gift to me. Thank you Henry for being a committed and loving father to your children, and opening the aperture of your heart to document how we have all grown, through your gift of photography. I have great admiration and gratitude for Santosh Sharma, who has shown me the power of being a woman of great faith. You have fed me when I needed to feel cared for, and blessed me with the reminder that holding sacred space day-to-day, be it in the kitchen, or wherever we stand, rests in keeping faith in all that is unseen by most, but provides the true sustenance for us all.

I remain in constant awe and gratitude
of what the human spirit is capable of manifesting,
when opened to the greater other dimensions of our being.

Acknowledgements

For information about our clinical practice,
distance consultations, and current workshops please go to our websites

www.integralhealth.ca
www.auricularmedicine.ca

Renascent Integral Health Centre
Co-founded by Alison & Mikhael Adams
54 Main Street East
Milton Ontario Canada
L9T 1N3

905.878.9994

ISBN 1425114873